Guide to the 1996 Presidential Election

Guide to the 1996 Presidential Election

Michael L. Goldstein

Congressional Quarterly Inc.
Washington, D.C. 20037

Congressional Quarterly Inc.

Congressional Quarterly Inc., an editorial research service and publishing company, serves clients in the fields of news, education, business, and government. It combines the specific coverage of Congress, government, and politics contained in the *Congressional Quarterly Weekly Report* with the more general subject range of an affiliated publication, *CQ Researcher.*

Congressional Quarterly also publishes a variety of books, including college political science textbooks under the CQ Press imprint and public affairs paperbacks on developing issues and events. CQ also publishes information directories and reference books on the federal government, national elections, and politics, including the *Guide to the Presidency,* the *Guide to Congress,* the *Guide to the U.S. Supreme Court,* the *Guide to U.S. Elections, Politics in America,* and *Congress A to Z: CQ's Ready Reference Encyclopedia.* The *CQ Almanac,* a compendium of legislation for one session of Congress, is published each year. *Congress and the Nation,* a record of government for a presidential term, is published every four years.

CQ publishes the *Congressional Monitor,* a daily report on current and future activities of congressional committees, and several newsletters including *Congressional Insight,* a weekly analysis of congressional action, and *Campaign Practices Reports,* a semimonthly update on campaign laws.

An electronic online information system, Washington Alert, provides immediate access to CQ's databases of legislative action, votes, schedules, profiles, and analyses.

Printed in the United States of America

Photo credits: cover—*St. Petersburg Times/Evening Independent*/Ricardo Ferro; p. xiv—AP/Wide World Photos; p. 18—*Charleston Gazette*/John F. Kennedy Library; p. 34—Reuters; p. 48—Fred Sons; p. 64—Jose R. Lopez/ NYT Pictures.

Library of Congress Cataloging-in-Publication Data

Goldstein, Michael L.
    Guide to the 1996 presidential election / Michael L. Goldstein.
        p.   cm.
    Includes bibliographical references and index.
    ISBN 0-87187-855-0
    1. Presidents—United States—Election—1996. I. Title.
JK526 1996   95-45596
324.973'0929—dc20   CIP

For Andy Goldstein, age nine,
who continues to weigh his options

Table of Contents

Tables and Figures

Tables

Figures

Preface

Although dramatic change in the presidential selection process may make for good reading, it does not necessarily make for easy writing. Given the rapid dissolution of the old electoral order, much of the 1992 version of this volume was outdated. Fashioning a new edition, however, was a major challenge because the framework of a new presidential selection process is unclear. I have tried to meet this challenge by writing a substantially new book focusing on a system that is in flux and that is moving rapidly away from a central role for the two major parties. I have also sought to maintain the original purpose of this book: to encourage and facilitate citizens' interest and participation in this process.

The *Guide to the 1996 Presidential Election* is a road map for understanding contemporary political change in the United States. It provides a new array of resources for this political journey, including references to Internet sites containing data on the presidential selection process. Like the previous volumes, this edition contains numerous charts and exercises as well as profiles of both major party and independent candidates who may play a role in the 1996 election.

This book would not have been possible without the help and support of many individuals. Dan Taylor helped locate appropriate Internet sites, Jason Linder provided invaluable computer assistance, and Ira Allen assisted in conceptualizing and writing the candidate profiles. Mark Bilsky and Rick Boylan at the Democratic National Committee, Michael Hess at the Republican National Committee, and Mike Dickerson of the public records office at the Federal Election Commission all graciously gave hours of their time in helping me understand the intricacies of contemporary party and FEC rules and regulations. Jeanne Ferris and Laura Carter of Congressional Quarterly patiently endured my constant efforts to turn a small book into a big one.

In all projects such as this, a few individuals take on special importance in providing inspiration and support, and they deserve special mention. Jack Pitney, my colleague at Claremont McKenna College, again served as an eager fount of information on virtually every aspect of the presidential selection process. Ron Elving, political editor at Congressional Quarterly, made delegate selection data available to me, even though doing so clearly complicated his busy schedule. Last but certainly not least, I want to express my deep appreciation to Susan Bales and Andy Goldstein, who tolerated the tremendous expense in time and energy that writing this book took from our family.

While I am grateful to all those whose efforts were turned to this undertaking, any errors or omissions are my own.

Guide to the 1996 Presidential Election

A moving van from Little Rock, Arkansas, parks in front of the White House January 20, 1993, as former Arkansas governor, now president, Bill Clinton moves in. Clinton was sworn in that day as the forty-second president of the United States.

The Changing Political Context

The United States has weathered a variety of social, economic, and political changes during its first two centuries that have influenced the way Americans select their chief executive. Virtually every aspect of the presidential selection process—from who votes to who is elected—has undergone a dramatic transformation.

In the late eighteenth century, the United States was newly formed, and many aspects of its political process, including presidential selection, reflected the imperatives of nation building. A small propertied elite that had led the revolt against England established a presidential selection process limited to participation by white propertied males. The process allowed its participants to manage conflict in an expansive new nation by giving them the power to select the top leadership without interference from the majority of Americans.

Suffrage was limited. African Americans were provided few rights of citizenship in most areas, and women were denied the vote in federal elections and generally in state and local elections as well. In most states, there were additional requirements restricting suffrage to white males who held property of a certain value or paid taxes of a certain amount. Only about 6 percent of the young nation's adult population in 1789 voted for presidential electors who chose George Washington, and no more than approximately 15 percent of all Americans

twenty-one years of age and over were considered qualified to vote in the first presidential elections.

Both those who were nominated and those who were elected in this early period accurately reflected the relatively closed nature of the presidential selection process. The first six presidents were members of prominent, upper-class families. Of the twenty-four candidates who received electoral votes in any of the first eight presidential elections, a majority were prominent political figures who had played a role in the American Revolution. Sixty-three percent had attended one of the Continental Congresses.

Much has changed in the presidential selection process since that time. Presidential candidates from the two major parties now are selected at national nominating conventions. Delegates to these conventions are either appointed by the political party or selected by voters in party primaries or caucuses. Other presidential candidates secure a spot on the general election ballot by direct nomination by local voters. The potential electorate is made up of virtually all citizens eighteen years of age or older—approximately 194 million Americans in November 1994.

The presidential candidates themselves, and their methods for reaching voters, have also changed (see Tables 1-1 and 1-2). Contemporary candidates include the humble, the once humble, and the always wealthy. To campaign among the ever-growing electorate, all are required to spend rapidly escalating sums over increasingly lengthy campaigns. These costs amounted to $550 million for all presidential candidates in 1992, compared with $500 million in 1988, $325 million in 1984, $275 million in 1980, $160 million in 1976, and $138 million in 1972. Although 1992 campaign costs were actually less in actual dollars than in 1988 because of the campaign's late start, the overall rate of increase over the last two decades far outstrips both the rising consumer price index and the increase in the number of voters (see Table 1-3).

All that remains of the original presidential selection process is the electoral college. As constitutionally established and as it functions today, the electoral college is the body that actually elects the president. While the names of electors have been removed from all but a handful of ballots, voters in the 1996 presidential election will still be casting their votes for slates of electors pledged to a presidential candidate. Two hundred years ago, electors were chosen by state legislatures or by those limited few who qualified to vote. The framers of the Constitution gave the members of the electoral college considerable leeway in making their selections. Although electors rarely do so, they still may exercise their individual choice for president irrespective of the popular vote. Since 1948 seven members of the electoral college have acted in this fashion and become "faithless electors."

Presidential Selection Methods

Although the contemporary presidential selection process is clearly distinct from the process that existed in the late eighteenth and early nineteenth centuries, the transformation was neither rapid nor direct. Furthermore, the change in this process is ongoing.

The Constitutional Plan

At least four distinct methods of presidential selection can be identified since the first

presidential election in 1789. The first method focused upon the electoral college as a deliberative body. States decided how their representatives to the electoral college were to be selected and were apportioned electors equal to their combined total of senators and representatives (a rule that continues today). Each elector would cast two votes to be divided between two candidates. The deliberations of the college resulted in the selection of a president (the individual receiving the most votes) and a vice president (the individual receiving the second largest vote). In case of a tie or if no candidate received a number of votes equal to a majority of the number of electors, the House of Representatives selected a president from among the top five candidates or from the top two candidates who tied.

By 1804 this original constitutional plan had been amended. The 1800 election produced a tie electoral vote, caused by confusion over who was a presidential candidate and who was a vice presidential candidate. The House ultimately selected Thomas Jefferson as president on February 17, 1801. The election prompted adoption of the Twelfth Amendment to the Constitution, which reduced the number of votes that each elector cast to one and formally established the practice of a president and vice president running together on a slate. If no candidate received the votes of a majority of electors, the House would select a president from among the top three candidates.

The Congressional Caucuses

The Twelfth Amendment codified a second presidential selection process that had begun in practice as early as 1800. By that year, members of Congress who identified with particular political parties were meeting in caucuses to nominate their party's presidential and vice presidential candidates. Meanwhile, state party leaders were nominating slates of electors pledged to those candidates. By 1824 qualified voters in eighteen of twenty-four states were voting directly for competing slates of electors.

The congressional caucus system of presidential selection, however, worked well only as long as interparty competition demanded intraparty discipline to nominate candidates and to carry on a campaign. With the demise of the Federalist Party by 1816, intraparty competition within the Democratic-Republican Party threatened the caucus system. In 1824 the Democratic-Republican congressional caucus, attended by a minority of the party's congressional delegation, nominated one candidate, while dissenting Democratic-Republicans nominated three other candidates through state legislatures or mass meetings. When none of the candidates received a majority in the electoral college, the House selected the president. The caucus system, already under attack for at least a decade, was thoroughly discredited. By 1840 all major political parties were holding national nominating conventions to select their presidential candidates.

The National Nominating Conventions

The rise of this third electoral method— national nominating conventions—was associated both with improved means of transportation and with the rapid democratization of the presidential selection process. Improvements in transportation, which enabled more citizens to attend the conventions, moved at lightning speed: In only one year, a trip from New York to Philadelphia was reduced from half a day by steamboat and rail to two hours by rail alone. Concurrently, the decline in voting restrictions for white males and the rise of citizen participation in the selection of presidential electors swelled the ranks of voters. In the election of 1824, the last presidential election in which a congressional caucus selected at least one of the candidates, the popular vote for president totaled less than 400,000. In the election of 1840, the first in which all major parties nominated their candidates at a national convention, the total popular vote topped 2.4 million (see Table 1-4). By 1848 all but one state selected presidential electors on the same day, reflecting both the increased popular and national

dimensions of the election. In general, these changes suggest the rapid transformation in the first half of the nineteenth century of the presidential selection process from a measured debate among sequestered elites to what one of the chants of the new popular politics identified as the "great commotion."

The national nominating convention remains a key feature of the political landscape. At national nominating conventions in Chicago and San Diego, the Democratic and Republican parties, respectively, will select their 1996 standard-bearers. However, the convention system that was established by the election of 1840 differs from later conventions in several respects.

First, all delegates to the early national nominating conventions were chosen directly by party leaders or at party gatherings. Most delegates to the Democratic and Republican conventions were selected by a state convention or by congressional district conventions, or both. Delegate selection, with few exceptions, was a matter left to the states or to state parties.

Second, for much of the nineteenth century, the formula for state representation at the conventions was fixed. From 1852 on, delegate representation at the Democratic convention was limited to twice the number of the state's senators and representatives. In 1860 Republicans adopted a comparable rule for state representation at their conventions. Irrespective of the strength of the party in a particular state, convention representation was set at four delegates at-large plus two delegates for each congressional district.

The control of delegate selection by party leaders in the early convention years made it difficult, if not counterproductive, for presidential aspirants to make appeals directly to delegates or to party rank and file. Indeed, until the initial convention system was altered beginning in 1904, the sole focus of presidential aspirants and the public was upon balloting at the convention. In a majority of cases where no incumbent was running, more than one ballot was needed to nominate a candidate.

Finally, beginning at their first national convention in 1832, Democrats established that two-thirds of all delegate votes be required for nomination. This rule essentially made party unity a precondition for nomination and gave minority factions within the party substantial veto power in the nominating process.

The Modified Convention System

The assault upon party dominance by progressives and the split Republican convention of 1912 (which led to an unsuccessful third-party candidacy by former president Theodore Roosevelt) were the catalysts to major changes in the presidential nominating conventions of the two major parties. They resulted in a fourth method of presidential selection—the modified convention system. Attempting to lessen the influence of party leaders upon the presidential selection process, progressives established a direct means for citizens to select delegates to the national convention or to express preferences for presidential aspirants: the presidential primary. By 1916 at least twenty states were holding presidential primaries, establishing this method of delegate selection as a regular feature of the political landscape.

The 1912 Republican convention also brought the issue of apportionment of delegates to a head. Delegates from southern states with few Republican voters had wielded considerable influence in the renomination of President William H. Taft. In the presidential election of 1908, the Democrats had won all ten southern states. In six of these states the Republican popular vote had been less than 30 percent of the total vote cast. Yet, at the 1912 Republican convention, the ten southern states had 228 delegate votes, more than 21 percent of the total delegate votes. Virtually all of these southern delegates voted for the renomination of Taft. For the 1916 party convention, Republicans put into effect a new arrangement that gave some recognition to local party strength in the apportionment of delegates. The Democrats followed with comparable rules beginning in 1944. This change was fueled in part by efforts of Southern Democrats to recoup influence lost when the two-thirds nominating rule was replaced by a simple majority in 1940.

Although the modifications in the presidential nominating conventions did not remove party leaders altogether from participation in the selection of nominees, they did open up alternative paths to nomination and bolstered the role of both the party rank and file and the public in the nomination process. One such alternative route involved gaining access to the media. Candidates who received attention from the print media and from the rapidly developing electronic media, especially television, could translate this coverage into primary votes and ultimately the nomination. For example, presidential candidate Wendell Willkie's close connections with two national periodicals (*Look* and *Fortune*) and Tennessee senator Estes Kefauver's extensive television coverage as chairman of the Senate Organized Crime Investigating Committee bolstered serious challenges to Republican and Democratic party leaders in 1940 and 1952, respectively.

A New Presidential Selection System?

Reform in delegate selection procedures and ongoing changes in the media have substantially altered the modified convention system. The role of third-party and independent presidential candidates has increased dramatically. Some observers say post-1968 changes have resulted in an entirely new presidential selection system.

The 1968 Democratic convention triggered a wave of internal party reforms related to the presidential selection process. In that year the Democrats nominated as their presidential candidate Vice President Hubert H. Humphrey. Humphrey had not formally entered a single primary because President Lyndon B. Johnson had been in the running. Johnson, however, withdrew unexpectedly from the campaign after the New Hampshire primary. Despite his absence from the primaries, Humphrey nonetheless received 67 percent of the total delegate votes at the convention. As a result, disgruntled Democrats who opposed Humphrey and disagreed with party leadership over a wide variety of domestic and foreign policy issues pushed for sweeping changes in the delegate selection process.

The product of this dissatisfaction was the McGovern-Fraser Commission report on delegate selection, which was adopted by the Democratic National Committee in 1971. Changes included abolishing the "unit rule," by which states could require their convention delegation to agree upon one candidate who would receive all of the delegation's votes; requiring the delegate selection process to occur the same year as the election; limiting the selection of delegates by state party committees; selecting at least 75 percent of a state's delegates at the congressional district level or below; and requiring affirmative efforts by each state to increase the delegate representation of minorities and women.

Additionally, the national Democratic Party adopted a charter in 1974 that significantly strengthened its power, at the expense of state party influence, to enforce the recent changes and other delegate selection procedures. Further Democratic rule making in 1976 banned winner-take-all and open primaries and mandated that delegates in each state be divided among candidates in proportion to the votes they received in Democratic caucuses or primaries. Finally, in 1980 the national Democratic Party adopted rules requiring all delegations to be equally divided among men and women and stipulating that all delegates selected through primaries or caucuses be officially pledged to a presidential candidate (or officially uncommitted) and bound for one convention ballot to that preference.

These changes produced a fundamentally new type of nominating convention marked by considerable rank and file influence in the Democratic delegate selection process and virtually no control over the process by party leaders or elected officials. Presidential primaries proliferated under the new rules, and party caucuses became more open to mass participation.

The immediate result was the selection in 1972 and 1976 of two "outsiders," South Dakota senator George McGovern and former Georgia governor Jimmy Carter. Neither would have been likely choices of conventions dominated by party leaders.

One unforeseen consequence of the new Democratic party rules was that they produced nominees who were either unelectable or, if elected, could not govern. In the first three general elections after the adoption of the new rules, Democratic nominees garnered an average of only 43 percent of the total vote and the Democrats' only successful candidate during this period, Jimmy Carter, struggled as president with the legislative wing of his own party. This problem, critics argued, was a product of the exclusion of important elements of the party from the nominating convention. For example, only 14 percent of Democratic senators and 15 percent of Democratic representatives participated as voting delegates at the 1980 Democratic convention, while a dozen years earlier, under the previous rules, 68 percent of the Democratic senators and 39 percent of Democratic representatives had participated as delegates.

A related complaint held that the proliferation of primaries forced candidates to start early and to compete for mass support in each state. This situation not only made winning the nomination an expensive exercise in political survival, but also opened up an increasingly public process to media scrutiny. In this regard, the party was losing control over its own deliberations as the media began to play a major role in the winnowing of candidates. The influence of party leaders in the selection of a nominee was thereby even further diminished.

Fueled by these complaints and a succession of defeated nominees, the Democratic party moved in the 1980s to balance earlier reforms with efforts to provide the national nominating convention more freedom from rank and file directives. By 1992 a new balance had been established. Substantial elements of earlier reforms remained, including a requirement that all delegations be equally divided between men and women and a ban on all winner-take-all or bonus schemes in the allocation of delegates. The Democratic rule makers additionally maintained a strict time frame for all delegate selection events. Democrats also moved away from earlier reforms, however, by facilitating the participation of party leaders and elected officials in the nominating convention. This was done by creating two new categories of delegates. The first included party and elected officials who would attend the convention by virtue of their elected or appointed positions. These delegates would be pledged to presidential candidates according to the caucus or primary votes of their respective states. The second category, primarily governors and members of Congress and the Democratic National Committee, would also be guaranteed delegate slots but would be officially unpledged. Finally, Democratic rule makers attempted to increase the deliberative potential of conventions by not binding delegates to vote for their original presidential preference on the first or any subsequent convention ballot. The election of Bill Clinton, the Democrats' first successful candidate in sixteen years, temporarily put to rest decades of internal party squabbles over delegate selection rules. As a result, delegate selection in 1996 will take place under rules that have the least number of changes in almost two decades.

The Republican Party has retained a much more federated structure than the Democratic Party and has never formally adopted delegate selection rules that are binding upon state parties. Nonetheless, changes in the Democratic rules have had an impact upon Republican procedures. Most importantly, Democratic-controlled state legislatures have often required Republicans as well as Democrats to conform to new delegate selection procedures. A case in point is the southern regional primary ("Super Tuesday") created in 1988. Initiated by Democratic-controlled state legislatures in order to bolster the chances of moderate Democratic presidential candidates, the new schedule of earlier primaries and caucuses throughout the region also applied to Republicans. Only after

they made substantial gains in state legislative races in November 1994 did Republicans regain the ability to control their own delegate selection procedures.

Despite a reluctance to mandate these procedures, Republicans have also been affected by the spirit of changes within the Democratic Party. Since 1964 at least three reform commissions have made suggestions on how the party's base could be broadened and the delegate selection process opened to new groups.

Third-party or independent presidential candidates also play an increasingly prominent role in the current presidential selection process. The vote for third-party candidates totaled almost 20 percent in 1992; even more votes are possible in 1996. As in the 1820s, when the old congressional caucus nominating system was in disrepair but not yet replaced by party nominating conventions, some presidential candidates are now nominated directly by supporters at the state level. In this regard, nomination at a major party convention is currently only one route to the general election ballot and potentially to the presidency.

The continuing changes in the presidential selection process have been fueled not only by the increasing democratization of American politics but also by technological change. The development of rail transportation, improved roads, popular newspapers, and the telegraph made national nominating conventions and national presidential elections possible. Similarly, the development of mass advertising, first through an independent press and later through radio and television, weakened the ability of political parties to monopolize political communication with voters. In this regard, this latest round of technological change is associated with the decline in support for the two major parties, the rise of candidate- rather than party-oriented campaigns, and the increasing ability of third-party or independent presidential candidates to communicate directly with voters.

With the aid of new and sophisticated technology, presidential candidates today communicate with an increasing number of Americans. Not only can candidates reach mass audiences through radio and television, but they can target their appeals to smaller and more select populations through direct mail, videotape technology, and the Internet. No less important, however, has been the impact of several decades of technological innovation on the costs of presidential campaigns. Although radio and television are an effective means of communicating with voters in an age of weak parties, they are also expensive. The new communications technology of the 1990s will also substantially boost campaign costs.

The overall result of these changes is that increasingly lengthy presidential campaigns, often beginning years before the election, cannot be won without millions of dollars. Despite campaign finance reform designed to level the financial playing field, the Republican and Democratic candidates who have raised the most money have received their party's nomination in every election but one since 1976. Lack of the requisite millions eliminated several prominent Republican candidates by early 1995—more than a year before the first caucus or primary vote would be cast in the election of 1996. The irony of the two-centuries-long democratization of the presidential selection process is that the increasing participation of Americans in that process, made possible because of a new and sophisticated communications technology, has made the resources of the wealthy and powerful only more indispensable.

Table 1-1 Backgrounds of U.S. Presidents

President	Age at first political office	First political office	Last political office[a]	Age at becoming president	State of residence[b]	Higher education[c]	Occupation
1. George Washington (1789–1797)	17	County surveyor	Presiding officer, Constitutional Convention	57	Va.	None	Farmer, surveyor
2. John Adams (1797–1801)	39	Surveyor of highways	Vice president	61	Mass.	Harvard	Farmer, lawyer
3. Thomas Jefferson (1801–1809)	26	State legislator	Vice president	58	Va.	William and Mary	Farmer, lawyer
4. James Madison (1809–1817)	25	State legislator	Secretary of state	58	Va.	Princeton	Farmer
5. James Monroe (1817–1825)	24	State legislator	Secretary of state	59	Va.	William and Mary	Farmer, lawyer
6. John Quincy Adams (1825–1829)	27	Minister to Netherlands	Secretary of state	58	Mass.	Harvard	Lawyer
7. Andrew Jackson (1829–1837)	21	Prosecuting attorney	U.S. Senate	62	Tenn.	None	Lawyer
8. Martin Van Buren (1837–1841)	30	Surrogate of county	Vice president	55	N.Y.	None	Lawyer
9. William Henry Harrison (1841)	26	Territorial delegate to Congress	Minister to Colombia	68	Ind.	Hampden-Sydney	Military
10. John Tyler (1841–1845)	21	State legislator	Vice president	51	Va.	William and Mary	Lawyer

11. James K. Polk (1845–1849)	28	State legislator	Governor	50	Tenn.	University of North Carolina	Lawyer
12. Zachary Taylor (1849–1850)	—	None	a	65	Ky.	None	Military
13. Millard Fillmore (1850–1853)	28	State legislator	Vice president	50	N.Y.	None	Lawyer
14. Franklin Pierce (1853–1857)	25	State legislator	U.S. district attorney	48	N.H.	Bowdoin	Lawyer
15. James Buchanan (1857–1861)	22	Assistant county prosecutor	Minister to Great Britain	65	Pa.	Dickinson	Lawyer
16. Abraham Lincoln (1861–1865)	25	State legislator	U.S. House of Representatives	52	Ill.	None	Lawyer
17. Andrew Johnson (1865–1869)	20	City alderman	Vice president	57	Tenn.	None	Tailor
18. Ulysses S. Grant (1869–1877)	—	None	a	47	Ohio	West Point	Military
19. Rutherford B. Hayes (1877–1881)	36	City solicitor	Governor	55	Ohio	Kenyon	Lawyer
20. James A. Garfield (1881)	28	State legislator	U.S. Senate	50	Ohio	Williams	Educator, lawyer
21. Chester Arthur (1881–1885)	31	State engineer	Vice president	51	N.Y.	Union	Lawyer
22. Grover Cleveland (1885–1889)	26	Assistant district attorney	Governor	48	N.Y.	None	Lawyer
23. Benjamin Harrison (1889–1893)	24	City attorney	U.S. Senate	56	Ind.	Miami of Ohio	Lawyer

Continued on next page

Table 1-1 *Continued*

President	Age at first political office	First political office[a]	Last political office[a]	Age at becoming president	State of residence[b]	Higher education[c]	Occupation
24. Grover Cleveland (1893–1897)	26	Assistant district attorney	U.S. president	52	N.Y.	None	Lawyer
25. William McKinley (1897–1901)	26	Prosecuting attorney	Governor	54	Ohio	Allegheny	Lawyer
26. Theodore Roosevelt (1901–1909)	24	State legislator	Vice president	42	N.Y.	Harvard	Lawyer, author
27. William H. Taft (1909–1913)	24	Assistant prosecuting attorney	Secretary of war	52	Ohio	Yale	Lawyer
28. Woodrow Wilson (1913–1921)	54	Governor	Governor	56	N.J.	Princeton	Educator
29. Warren G. Harding (1921–1923)	35	State legislator	U.S. Senate	56	Ohio	Ohio Central	Newspaper editor
30. Calvin Coolidge (1923–1929)	26	City councilman	Vice president	51	Mass.	Amherst	Lawyer
31. Herbert Hoover (1929–1933)	43	Relief and food administrator	Secretary of commerce	55	Calif.	Stanford	Mining engineer
32. Franklin D. Roosevelt (1933–1945)	28	State legislator	Governor	49	N.Y.	Harvard	Lawyer
33. Harry S. Truman (1945–1953)	38	County judge (commissioner)	Vice president	61	Mo.	None	Clerk, store owner

President	Age	First office	Last office before presidency[a]	Age	State[b]	Education[c]	Occupation
34. Dwight D. Eisenhower (1953–1961)	—	None	[a]	63	Kan.	West Point	Military
35. John F. Kennedy (1961–1963)	29	U.S. House of Representatives	U.S. Senate	43	Mass.	Harvard	Newspaper reporter
36. Lyndon B. Johnson (1963–1969)	28	U.S. House of Representatives	Vice president	55	Texas	Southwest Texas State Teacher's College	Educator
37. Richard Nixon (1969–1974)	29	Office of Price Administration	Vice president	56	Calif.	Whittier	Lawyer
38. Gerald R. Ford (1974–1977)	36	U.S. House of Representatives	Vice president	61	Mich.	University of Michigan	Lawyer
39. Jimmy Carter (1977–1981)	38	County Board of Education	Governor	52	Ga.	U.S. Naval Academy	Farmer, businessman
40. Ronald Reagan (1981–1989)	55	Governor	Governor	69	Calif.	Eureka	Entertainer
41. George Bush (1989–1993)	42	U.S. House of Representatives	Vice president	64	Texas	Yale	Businessman
42. Bill Clinton (1993–)	31	State attorney general	Governor	46	Ark.	Georgetown	Lawyer

Sources: Richard A. Watson and Norman C. Thomas, *The Politics of the Presidency*, 2d ed. (Washington, D.C.: CQ Press, 1988), 515–519; and *Presidential Elections, 1789–1992* (Washington, D.C.: Congressional Quarterly Inc., 1995).

[a] This category refers to the last civilian office held before the presidency. Taylor, Grant, and Eisenhower had served as generals before becoming president.
[b] The state identified is the primary residence of the president during his adult years, not necessarily where he was born.
[c] Refers to undergraduate education.

Table 1-2   Presidential Selection: A Historical Review

Election year	Winning candidate	Means of selection
1789	George Washington	Original constitutional plan
1792	George Washington	Original constitutional plan
1796	John Adams	Congressional caucus
1800	Thomas Jefferson	Congressional caucus
1804	Thomas Jefferson	Congressional caucus
1808	James Madison	Congressional caucus
1812	James Madison	Congressional caucus
1816	James Monroe	Congressional caucus
1820	James Monroe	Congressional caucus
1824	John Quincy Adams	State legislatures
1828	Andrew Jackson	State conventions, mass meetings, and state legislatures
1832	Andrew Jackson	National convention
1836	Martin Van Buren	National convention
1840	William Henry Harrison	National convention
1844	James K. Polk	National convention
1848	Zachary Taylor	National convention
1852	Franklin Pierce	National convention
1856	James Buchanan	National convention
1860	Abraham Lincoln	National convention
1864	Abraham Lincoln	National convention
1868	Ulysses S. Grant	National convention
1872	Ulysses S. Grant	National convention
1876	Rutherford B. Hayes	National convention
1880	James A. Garfield	National convention
1884	Grover Cleveland	National convention
1888	Benjamin Harrison	National convention
1892	Grover Cleveland	National convention
1896	William McKinley	National convention
1900	William McKinley	National convention
1904	Theodore Roosevelt	National convention
1908	William H. Taft	National convention
1912	Woodrow Wilson	Modified national convention
1916	Woodrow Wilson	Modified national convention
1920	Warren G. Harding	Modified national convention
1924	Calvin Coolidge	Modified national convention
1928	Herbert Hoover	Modified national convention
1932	Franklin D. Roosevelt	Modified national convention
1936	Franklin D. Roosevelt	Modified national convention
1940	Franklin D. Roosevelt	Modified national convention
1944	Franklin D. Roosevelt	Modified national convention
1948	Harry S. Truman	Modified national convention
1952	Dwight D. Eisenhower	Modified national convention
1956	Dwight D. Eisenhower	Modified national convention
1960	John F. Kennedy	Modified national convention
1964	Lyndon B. Johnson	Modified national convention
1968	Richard Nixon	Modified national convention

Table 1-2 *Continued*

Election year	Winning candidate	Means of selection
1972	Richard Nixon	Modified national convention
1976	Jimmy Carter	Modified national convention
1980	Ronald Reagan	Modified national convention
1984	Ronald Reagan	Modified national convention
1988	George Bush	Modified national convention
1992	Bill Clinton	Modified national convention

Table1-3 Presidential Spending and Votes, 1960–1992

Year	Actual spending (in millions of dollars)	CPI (1960 = 100)	Adjusted spending (in millions of dollars)	Votes cast (in millions)
1960	30.0	100.0	30.0	68.8
1964	60.0	104.7	57.3	70.6
1968	100.0	117.5	85.1	73.2
1972	138.0	141.2	97.7	77.7
1976	160.0	192.2	83.2	81.6
1980	275.0	278.1	98.9	86.5
1984	325.0	346.8	93.7	92.7
1988	500.0	385.4	126.5	91.6
1992	550.0	446.9	117.8	104.4

Sources: Herbert E. Alexander and Anthony Corrado, *Financing the 1992 Election* (Armonk, N.Y.: M.E. Sharpe, 1995), 21; and *Presidential Elections, 1789–1992* (Washington, D.C.: Congressional Quarterly Inc., 1995).

Note: CPI = consumer price index.

Table 1-4 Voter Participation in Presidential Elections

Election year and winning candidate	Population of voting age	Voters	Percentage of voting-age population voting
1828 Andrew Jackson	5,201,000	1,155,000	22.2
1832 Andrew Jackson	5,914,000	1,218,000	20.6
1836 Martin Van Buren	6,710,000	1,505,000	22.4
1840 William Henry Harrison	7,566,000	2,412,000	31.9
1844 James K. Polk	8,840,000	2,701,000	30.6
1848 Zachary Taylor	10,081,000	2,879,000	28.6
1852 Franklin Pierce	11,582,000	3,162,000	27.3
1856 James Buchanan	13,235,000	4,045,000	30.6
1860 Abraham Lincoln	14,880,000	4,690,000	31.5
1864 Abraham Lincoln	16,450,000	4,011,000	24.4
1868 Ulysses S. Grant	18,019,000	5,720,000	31.7
1872 Ulysses S. Grant	20,176,000	6,460,000	32.0
1876 Rutherford B. Hayes	22,724,000	8,422,000	37.1

Continued on next page

Table 1-4   *Continued*

Election year and winning candidate	Population of voting age	Voters	Percentage of voting-age population voting
1880 James A. Garfield	25,462,000	9,217,000	36.2
1884 Grover Cleveland	28,275,000	10,053,000	35.6
1888 Benjamin Harrison	31,377,000	11,383,000	36.3
1892 Grover Cleveland	34,522,000	12,061,000	34.9
1896 William McKinley	37,745,000	13,907,000	36.8
1900 William McKinley	41,077,000	13,968,000	34.0
1904 Theodore Roosevelt	45,498,000	13,531,000	29.7
1908 William H. Taft	49,919,000	14,884,000	29.8
1912 Woodrow Wilson	53,830,000	15,037,000	27.9
1916 Woodrow Wilson	57,708,000	18,531,000	32.1
1920 Warren G. Harding	62,988,000	26,748,000	42.5
1924 Calvin Coolidge	66,414,000	29,086,000	43.8
1928 Herbert Hoover	71,185,000	36,812,000	51.7
1932 Franklin D. Roosevelt	75,768,000	39,759,000	52.5
1936 Franklin D. Roosevelt	80,174,000	45,655,000	56.9
1940 Franklin D. Roosevelt	84,728,000	49,900,000	58.9
1944 Franklin D. Roosevelt	85,654,000	47,977,000	56.0
1948 Harry S. Truman	95,573,000	48,794,000	51.1
1952 Dwight D. Eisenhower	99,929,000	61,551,000	61.6
1956 Dwight D. Eisenhower	104,515,000	62,027,000	59.3
1960 John F. Kennedy	109,672,000	68,838,000	63.1
1964 Lyndon B. Johnson	114,090,000	70,645,000	61.9
1968 Richard Nixon	120,285,000	73,212,000	60.9
1972 Richard Nixon	140,777,000	77,719,000	55.2
1976 Jimmy Carter	152,308,000	81,556,000	53.5
1980 Ronald Reagan	164,595,000	86,515,000	52.6
1984 Ronald Reagan	174,468,000	92,653,000	53.1
1988 George Bush	182,779,000	91,595,000	50.1
1992 Bill Clinton	189,044,000	104,423,000	55.2

Sources: Bureau of the Census, *Nonvoting,* Series P-23, No. 102 (Washington, D.C.: U.S. Government Printing Office, 1980); *Presidential Elections, 1789–1992* (Washington, D.C.: Congressional Quarterly Inc., 1995); and Committee for the Study of the American Electorate.

Note: Data prior to 1828 excluded because of the absence of popular elections for presidential electors in many states and the failure to record results in states where popular elections were held. Percentages are based on figures that have been rounded.

Exercises

1. Simulate a meeting of the electoral college in the late eighteenth century. Most electors have been selected by their state legislatures with no popular balloting for presidential aspirants. Each elector has two votes, which must be divided between two candidates. Several candidates have expressed an interest in the presidency and several others in the vice presidency. The top vote-getter will be elected president and the runner-up elected vice president. If no candidate receives a number of votes equal to a majority of electors, the president will be selected by the House of Representatives from the top five candidates. Each state delegation in the House has only one vote. The candidate with the most votes (and a majority) is elected.

Compare this process with the present operation of the electoral college. Is it more or less democratic? Does it produce better or worse presidents?

2. Compare the presidential selection process in the United States in the late eighteenth century with that of the selection of the chief executive in a present-day "new nation" in either Africa or Asia.

3. Most changes in the presidential selection process have been prompted by the dissatisfaction of presidential aspirants with the existing process. For example, the rise of alternative nominating mechanisms to the congressional caucus stemmed from the dissatisfaction of candidates rejected by the caucus. The increasing use of new delegate allocation schemes in the 1970s and 1980s was related to the failure of particular candidates to use the old mechanisms to their advantage. What comparable situations in the near future can be envisioned that would lead to further changes?

4. Technological change has often had a direct impact upon the presidential selection process. For example, improved transportation made national nominating conventions possible and television ultimately changed the way voters evaluate candidates. Identify one major technological change in American history and chart its impact upon presidential elections.

5. Significant increases in voter participation in presidential elections have related to particular historical and political events. For example, the increase in voter participation in the 1920 presidential election reflected the votes of newly enfranchised women (see Table 1-4).

Review the trends in voting participation and identify possible political and historical events that might explain these trends. Why were turnouts comparatively high in 1840, 1876, 1960, and 1992? Voter participation in presidential elections has been significantly lower in the last several decades than in the 1950s and 1960s. What might explain this downturn? Would this trend be expected to continue?

6. Voter participation rates in American presidential elections have consistently lagged behind elections in other Western democracies. Compare the election process of another Western democracy with that of the United States. What might explain the differences in voter participation in the two nations?

7. Clear channels of mobility to the presidency exist. Successful presidential aspirants are more likely to reside in particular states and are more likely to have held particular appointed or elected positions (see Table 1-1).

Using data included in this chapter, compare early patterns of mobility to the presidency (1789–1824) with those since 1945. What might account for any differences? What patterns of mobility could be expected in the near future? Why?

Additional Sources
Printed Material and Videos

Fisher, Roger. *Tippecanoe and Trinkets Too.* Urbana: University of Illinois Press, 1988. A delightful analysis of the changes in the presidential selection process through a review of campaign memorabilia.

Kelly, Kate. *Election Day: An American Holiday, An American History.* New York: Facts on File, 1991. A novel treatment of the changing style of American elections through a focus on election day.

Presidential Elections, 1789–1992. Washington, D.C.: Congressional Quarterly Inc., 1995. Includes a succinct but informed historical review of presidential elections through 1992 with considerable documentation.

Rose, Gary L., ed. *Controversial Issues in Presidential Selection.* Albany: State University of New York Press, 1994. Presents debates on eleven issues related to the presidential selection process that focus both on the overall characteristics of the system and specific components of the system, such as the mass media.

On-Line Data

"The Nation's Forum." This Library of Congress site provides access to fifty-nine early sound recordings of national leaders from 1918 to 1920, including candidates and other politicians involved in the 1920 presidential election campaign. Users may both search the database for particular personalities and download audio segments.
Access method: World Wide Web
To access: http://lcweb2.loc.gov/nfhome. html
Choose: From War to Normalcy

Sen. John F. Kennedy, a Roman Catholic, campaigns in predominantly Protestant West Virginia in 1960. His triumph in the West Virginia Democratic primary proved that he would be a viable national candidate if selected by party leaders.

2

The Preliminaries

The race for the presidency usually starts long before the national conventions or the primaries or caucuses take place. Potential aspirants may drop hints about running or an incumbent president may use the powers or resources of office with a reelection bid in mind. Indeed, the preliminaries of a presidential election campaign can begin almost as soon as the returns from the previous campaign have been tabulated.

Multiyear campaigns have been prompted both by changes in the laws and procedures governing major party candidates and by the appearance of prominent candidates who operate outside the constraints of major party politics and federal campaign finance laws. Although high public support for the Bush administration during and immediately after the Persian Gulf War delayed the start of the 1992 campaign, the 1996 campaign reflects many of the new characteristics of the presidential selection process.

The Multiyear Campaign

While direct participation of party rank and file in the nomination of major party candidates through primaries has been a characteristic of the presidential selection process since 1904, only in the last two decades has it become the preferred method of delegate selection. In 1968 less than 40 percent of all con-

vention delegates were chosen via primaries. By 1976 this figure had topped 70 percent (see Table 2-1). In the last decade rank and file participation in the party caucuses also has been bolstered by changes in party rules that prevent undue manipulation by party officials. As a result, candidates now need the support of numerous primary voters and caucus participants throughout the nation. In the past, major party candidates entered a select number of primaries not because winning delegates would assure them the nomination but to prove to party leaders that they were potentially electable. Sen. John F. Kennedy, a Roman Catholic, entered and won the 1960 Democratic primary in predominantly Protestant West Virginia, making the point that he would be a viable national candidate if selected by party leaders. Now, rank and file primary and caucus participants control the major party nominations.

Given this critical change in the presidential selection process, candidates must establish early their own base of core supporters and then rely to a large degree upon the mass media to reach the disparate groups of voters who now participate in party primaries and caucuses. With the elimination of party leaders from the center of the nomination process, candidates are required to craft a favorable national image that takes time and careful planning to create.

The increasing role of the media therefore has been one key catalyst to longer campaigns. Reaching many new participants in the presidential selection process through the mass media requires more time and money than merely negotiating with a select number of party leaders. Furthermore, the mass media tend to focus on candidates they consider front-runners or contenders. Candidates thus must first convince the media, even before any votes are cast, that they are electable. Early electoral success in the campaign also becomes a prerequisite to further press coverage. Most major party nominees have won or far surpassed media expectations in the Iowa caucuses and New Hampshire primary—the media-created "fishbowls" of the early delegate selection process. The key to success for candidates is not necessarily winning but gaining favorable media coverage; this was evident in the 1992 New Hampshire primary when President George Bush handily defeated challenger Pat Buchanan but was defined by the media as a weakened incumbent. On the Democratic side, a distant second place finish by the former front-runner, Arkansas governor Bill Clinton, made him "the comeback kid," a self-characterization the media readily adapted. In other campaign events in which no delegates are selected, the media also have played an increasingly critical role in determining "winners" and "losers." In essence, the new media-based imperatives require candidates to spend years preparing for campaigns that may well end as soon as any delegates to the national conventions are chosen.

Additionally, the major parties themselves have placed a premium on early starts by candidates. Prior to major party reforms in the early 1970s, delegates to national nominating conventions were largely selected by party leaders or party conventions over a period of several years. Beginning in 1972, this process was opened significantly to rank and file participation and limited to several months, beginning with the Iowa caucuses and the New Hampshire primary in February and ending with a round of primaries and state conventions in early June of the election year. Additional "front loading" (selecting increased numbers of delegates earlier in this shortened time frame) has further accelerated the delegate selection process within this brief period. Since more than a dozen states have moved up their primary or caucus dates for 1996, the majority of delegates to both the Democratic and Republican nominating conventions will be selected in the shortest period of time since delegate selection procedures to national nominating conventions have been documented—in approximately a one-month period in February and March of 1996.

Finally, the Federal Election Campaign Act, administered by the Federal Election Commission (FEC), has served to extend campaigns by rewarding major party candidates who start early. To receive matching funds on January 1 of the election year, a candidate must have raised more than $100,000 by collecting more than $5,000 in twenty different states in amounts no greater than $250 from any individual contributor. After qualifying for these funds, candidates must conform both to specific campaign expenditure limits in every state and to a nationwide expenditure limit. Individual contributions to publicly funded candidates in the primary election process are limited to $1,000 and group contributions are limited to $5,000; only the first $250 of any individual contribution is matched by public funds. In sum, the act has required that presidential aspirants establish networks of core supporters early in the nomination process to take full advantage of its public financing provisions. Federal matching funds provided to candidates in 1992 are listed in Table 2-2.

The act also encourages major party candidates to begin their campaigns years in advance by punishing losers and rewarding winners at an early stage in the delegate selection process. Even though only a fraction of delegates are chosen at a single primary, the law eliminates matching funds for any candidate who receives less than 10 percent of the vote in two consecutive primaries. To requalify for public funding, the candidate must receive 20 percent of the vote in a later primary. With the elimination of public funds, private funding for the "losing" candidate becomes problematic.

Third-party and independent candidates operate within a somewhat different strategic context during the campaign preliminaries. Most do not compete in primaries or caucuses and many do not depend on a convention for nomination. Access to the general election ballot is generally secured through a state-by-state petition process. Money and organization are clearly important in funding local activities to support their candidacies, but these candidates generally operate outside the public funding opportunities or constraints of the Federal Election Campaign Act. Most do not qualify as a political party under the law or decide not to participate. Ross Perot, the most successful independent candidate since Theodore Roosevelt in 1912, sought neither matching funds during the 1992 campaign preliminaries nor general election funding even after he received the requisite 5 percent of the vote in November.

Despite these differences, independent and third-party candidates are significantly affected by the campaign preliminaries of the major parties. Their ability both to secure a place on the ballot and ultimately to compete in November depends largely upon the satisfaction of major party voters with their own nominees. No less important is whether the media consider independent or minor party candidates to be viable alternatives worthy of coverage.

In sum, the conventional wisdom of the new campaign preliminaries, as of 1992, was that candidates must start early to raise funds, develop a base of core supporters, and pursue a positive public image to win a major party nomination. To survive the early formative stage of the process, candidates must be declared contenders by both the press and the FEC to bring sufficient momentum to the Iowa caucuses and the New Hampshire primary. A strong showing in either of these events force-

fully moves the campaign into the later caucuses and primaries by providing it national credibility.

Some of this wisdom was confirmed by the 1992 campaign. The eventual party nominees raised the most money and clearly had the strongest organizational bases by the time the delegate selection process began. Candidates who faltered early did so as a result of lackluster fund raising, negative or minimal media coverage, and critical caucus or primary losses.

Much of this wisdom, however, was not confirmed. The 1992 presidential campaign started slower than any campaign in almost two decades. By June 30, 1991, only one candidate had decided to challenge President Bush (see Table 2-3). Furthermore, some candidates who scored early electoral successes still engendered either negative or mixed media coverage. For example, victories by Sen. Tom Harkin, D-Iowa, and former senator Paul Tsongas, D-Mass., in the Iowa caucuses and New Hampshire primary, respectively, gave each of their campaigns only a minimal boost. An independent candidate entered the race, dropped out, re-entered, and still received almost 20 percent of the vote in the general election. And Clinton, the eventual Democratic nominee, overcame a series of extensive media exposés focusing on his personal life to win his party's nomination and to be elected president.

Some of the distinct dynamics of campaign preliminaries in 1992 were clearly derived from the unusual domestic political atmosphere during and immediately after the Gulf War. Public preoccupation with the war and high support for President Bush delayed the beginning of the campaign and discouraged several potential candidates from entering. Once the campaign did begin, however, other factors fueled new dynamics; for example, the continuing public decline in major party loyalty and the increasing efforts of candidates to avoid traditional news formats or circumvent the traditional media by using new communications technologies further prompted new patterns of campaign preliminaries. One candidate actually declared his candidacy on a national television "call-in" program.

The result was more a politics of personality in which major party nominees are no longer required to broker broad party coalitions or secure relatively unblemished media images to win the nomination. In a potentially new era of American presidential elections, what would formerly have been considered a damaging pre-election campaign may now be sufficient to win both major party nomination and the presidency.

New Campaign Preliminaries

In order to successfully navigate a pre-general election campaign that involves rank and file voters, grants a major winnowing role to the mass media, and requires virtually all major party candidates to conform to the fund-raising requirements and expenditure limits of the Federal Election Campaign Act, candidates have both participated in and initiated an increasing number of campaign preliminaries. These include general efforts to mold public perception of the campaign and specific party- or interest group-sponsored events in which candidates have the opportunity to appear or compete. While none of these is directly related to the selection of delegates to national nominating conventions, each nevertheless has a significant impact on the success both of major party candidates in securing the nomination and on the viability of minor party or independent candidates.

The 1996 preliminaries on the Republican side reflect this. By early 1995 conventional wisdom, supplied by Republican front- runners Sen. Bob Dole, R-Kan., and Sen. Phil Gramm, R-Texas, and generally accepted by the media, stressed that the nomination could not be won without raising $20 million by the end of the year. Although debatable and untested, this assertion had significant impact.

Several potential Republican candidates, such as Richard Cheney, Jack Kemp, and former vice president Dan Quayle, decided such a fund-raising burden was too great and declined to enter the race. Other Republican candidates were forced to emphasize that they were competitive in the money race or risk being ignored by the press and the public. In April, Lamar Alexander, former governor of Tennessee, reminded his followers that even though he was behind Dole and Gramm, he was still ahead of President Bush's position at a comparable time in the 1988 campaign. California governor Pete Wilson countered rumors that his 1994 gubernatorial campaign had depleted his fund-raising sources by revealing to reporters in May that he already had $8 million in pledges of financial support.

Candidates have also attempted to generate images of growing public support through public endorsements by key organizational heads or other politicians. For example, in early April of 1995, the entire New York Republican congressional delegation endorsed Dole—a story and photo opportunity that was certainly not missed by his campaign. Candidates also increasingly use public opinion polls to bolster positive public perception or to raise questions about their opponents' viability. This often involves what one national pollster labels "happy polling," in which the candidate's pollsters cast their public opinion net so widely and loosely that at least some good news is ensured.

Polling by candidates is supplemented by extensive public opinion research by the television networks and news magazines. Releases of these polls become campaign events that mold public perception. Given that most of these early polls reflect little more than name recognition, they tend to bolster the campaigns of highly visible politicians or personalities, prompting other candidates to look for good news in their own polling.

The second category of increasingly important campaign preliminaries includes events sponsored by local Democratic or Republican parties or by a variety of nonparty groups that wish to be wooed by candidates. In some cases, votes or "straw polls" are taken among the audience. These events serve as forums for candidates to reveal their platforms and to provide them necessary visibility, which is especially critical for candidates of the party not controlling the White House, who usually have difficulty competing for press coverage with a sitting president.

In 1991 and early 1992, candidate forums provided critical opportunities for Democratic contenders to be heard by both party regulars and the media. Straw polls conducted among delegates at the Florida Democratic Convention in December 1991 and the California Republican Convention in early March 1992 helped showcase Clinton as the Democratic front-runner and provided Bush needed support to fend off a challenge by television commentator Buchanan.

Candidate forums and straw polls promise to play an even larger role in the 1996 preliminaries. By the end of June 1995, Republican candidates had already participated in forums sponsored by the New Hampshire Republican Party and the Midwest Republican Leadership Conference and competed in straw polls sponsored by the Republican parties in California, Iowa, Louisiana, Oklahoma, South Carolina, Texas, and Virginia. Straw polls are also planned on the municipal level, with at least fifteen cities holding nonbinding candidate referendums in conjunction with their municipal elections in November 1995.

One new twist for the 1996 preliminaries was the attendance of representatives of President Clinton and every possible Republican challenger at Ross Perot's August 1995 meeting of his United We Stand organization. Not only did this provide a national forum for media-hungry candidates but it also projected Perot into the national limelight again.

Candidates are also increasingly willing to debate each other to gain possible positive media coverage. Televised debates offer candidates the opportunity to reach millions of voters. They provide free media exposure and a chance for candidates to outshine opponents and test new themes and styles. The cost, how-

ever, may be a losing performance that damages the campaign. Public responses to candidate performances are carefully assessed by campaigns, because once perceptions are established they are often difficult to change. For example, the performance of Democratic candidate Bruce E. Babbitt in the early debates in 1987 reflected a style that one campaign consultant identified as "a cross between Jimmy Stewart and Richard Nixon." Not surprisingly, Babbitt later accepted an invitation to appear in a skit on "Saturday Night Live" to change this image.

The increasing need to engage in campaign preliminaries while simultaneously conforming to the guidelines of the Federal Election Campaign Act, which go into effect once a candidate formally declares, has prompted major party candidates to establish ways to campaign without being official candidates (see Table 2-4). One solution has been to delay declaring candidacy and use a political action committee (PAC) to support campaign activities. This approach, first pioneered by precandidate Ronald Reagan in preparation for the 1980 campaign, has become increasingly popular. While the use of PACs for this purpose declined in the 1992 campaign, perhaps due to a long period in which President Bush was viewed as invincible, their popularity as precampaign vehicles has re-emerged for the 1996 campaign. Seven of ten Republican candidates who had declared through August of 1995 had current or recent affiliations with PACs.

Another solution is the use of tax-exempt foundations as precampaign vehicles. Unregulated by the FEC, these foundations have far fewer disclosure requirements and therefore do not have to publicly identify contributors. Associates of Bob Dole in 1994 established the Better America Foundation, a social welfare organization under section 501(c)(4) of the Internal Revenue Code, which has broadcast advertisements favorable to Dole. Speaker of the House and potential presidential candidate Newt Gingrich, R-Ga., has long been associated with the

Progress and Freedom Foundation, which supports an array of educational activities with Gingrich at the center. As a charitable foundation under section 501(c)(3) of the Internal Revenue Code, it provides donors a tax deduction for their contributions.

Virtually all of the new preliminaries reflect the growing importance of the media. Candidates desperately need media exposure. In providing this exposure, however, the media ultimately comment and interpret. And, as one observer facetiously put it, "What the media giveth, it [*sic*] can taketh away." The 1992 campaign may have altered conventional notions as to exactly where and when the media are most influential, but it also reaffirmed the overall critical role the media now perform in the presidential nominating process and prompted candidates to search for ways to avoid constant media scrutiny.

The 1996 campaign promises more of the same. Sen. Phil Gramm's campaign was shaken early on by a media exposé that he had invested money in the production of a pornographic movie. Pete Wilson, a leading spokesman on immigration issues, has been charged by the media with employing an illegal alien. In this regard, there is no doubt that the media will be an important actor in the 1996 preliminaries, but exactly in what circumstances and through what means candidates will be able to avoid media control of the campaign will only become clear as the overall outline of a quickly changing presidential selection process emerges.

1996 Delegate Selection Rules

Just as the road to the convention has become long and torturous, so have the rules for the selection of delegates to major party conventions become increasingly complex. New delegate selection rules adopted by the Democratic National Committee in 1990 and 1994 furthered this trend by balancing earlier delegate selection reforms that emphasized rank and file control of the process with a new

emphasis on increased participation by elected and appointed Democratic Party officials (see Table 2-5). The basic Democratic rules governing delegate selection for 1996 are:

• Primaries and caucuses must be held between the first Tuesday in March and second Tuesday in June of 1996, with some exceptions (see Table 2-6).

• Delegates are not formally bound to candidates but "in all good conscience should reflect the sentiments of those who elected them."

• Candidates must receive 15 percent of the statewide primary or caucus votes to be allocated statewide delegates.

• In both primary and caucus states, candidates must receive 15 percent of the vote in a particular district to be allocated district delegates.

• Seventy-five percent of the base allocation of delegates to each state (the total state delegation minus pledged or unpledged party officials) must be elected at the congressional district level.

• Each state delegation will be supplemented by an additional 15 percent. These additional delegate slots will be apportioned to local party officials who will be pledged delegates. Each state delegation will also be supplemented by delegate slots filled by present or former national party leaders. These delegates are officially unpledged.

• All delegations to the convention must be equally divided between men and women.

For the Democrats, the changes from 1992 to 1996 in the rules governing delegate selection are relatively minor. Loophole and bonus allocation schemes, which reward winning candidates with additional delegates, are again prohibited. The continuing emphasis on the equal division of convention delegations between men and women is upheld with the specification that district-level delegates, who are selected before at-large delegates, must conform to this rule. All state delegations are again expanded by 15 percent to ensure inclusion of party officials, and approximately 18 percent of all convention slots are again allocated to present and former national party officials who will attend as formerly unpledged delegates (or, as the media have labeled them, "superdelegates"). The president and vice president (if Democrats), all former chairs of the Democratic National Committee, and all Democratic members of Congress are now automatically included as unpledged delegates. This precludes the necessity in 1996 for either House or Senate Democrats to meet in order to select their delegates. Democrats also added to the delegate selection rules provisions that lower the barriers on the state level to securing access to the primary ballot.

The Republicans' rules for the selection and allocation of delegates to their national convention have also changed, but they reflect much more continuity than the ever-changing Democratic rules. Given the more decentralized nature of the Republican Party, few delegate selection procedures have been mandated. In contrast to the Democrats, the Republicans have not set a strict time frame for all primaries and caucuses and have not banned winner-take-all statewide primaries or the election of all state delegates on a statewide basis. Additionally, state Republican parties may set their own rules in binding delegates according to the preferences of Republican voters in primaries or caucuses.

As a result of these differences, Republican and Democratic delegate selection in 1996 will proceed at a slightly different pace, with Republicans beginning to select delegates about two weeks before Democrats and utilizing primaries to select delegates more often than Democrats. The Republicans also will permit a greater variety of mechanisms for allocating delegates based on primary or caucus results.

In sum, the delegate selection process for 1996 will follow a myriad of distinct party rules. For example, on February 20, 1996, both New Hampshire Republicans and Democrats will hold their parties' first primaries of the delegate selection season. The similarity, however, ends there. On the Republican side, all sixteen delegates will be allotted proportionally, based on the statewide vote. To receive delegates, a candidate's vote must total at least 10 percent statewide. Delegates are pledged to their original presidential preference unless that candidate withdraws.

On the Democratic side, thirteen delegates will be elected on a congressional district basis, while four will be elected statewide. District delegates will be allotted proportionally on the basis of the district vote, while statewide delegates will be apportioned on the basis of the statewide vote. In each case, a candidate must receive at least 15 percent of the vote to be allotted delegates. In addition, district delegates will select three other delegates, who are pledged to candidates in proportion to the statewide primary vote. These delegate positions are reserved for state and local elected officials such as statewide officers, mayors, or state legislative leaders. Finally, six other unpledged delegates will be selected as part of the New Hampshire delegation to the Democratic National Convention; these will include members of the Democratic National Committee who reside in New Hampshire, Democratic members of Congress from New Hampshire, the governor (if he or she is a Democrat), and distinguished former Democratic officeholders who reside in New Hampshire. With the exception of the officially unpledged delegates, all delegates are required "in all good conscience" to reflect the sentiments of the voters who elected them.

For minor parties that have qualified as recognized political parties in New Hampshire, February 20, 1996, will also be primary day. For independent candidates, access to the general election ballot involves a petition process that requires the submission of the signatures of three thousand legal voters by August 7.

The road to nomination is long and complex. Independent and minor party candidates are dependent upon fifty distinct sets of rules to qualify for the general election ballot. Major party candidates are subject both to a complex array of rules governing the allocation of delegates and to the evaluation of more than fifty electorates throughout the primary and caucus process. Nonetheless, individual steps in the nominating process may be exaggerated, and, indeed, state parties frequently change their primary or caucus dates with the hope that they might have a greater impact upon the presidential selection process. The best example of this is the disproportionate role of the Iowa caucuses and the New Hampshire primary. With less than 2 percent of the national population, these states hold early major party delegate selection events that receive considerable media scrutiny and often set the tone of the entire nomination process. In 1988 more than one-third of the preconvention national media coverage focused on these states. While media cov-

erage of these early delegate selection events declined in 1992, in part because the Iowa caucuses were uncontested, they nonetheless remained grossly overrepresented in news coverage in relation to both the states' populations and delegates selected.

The race for the presidency, however, reaches truly national proportions only in late summer of the election year. At that time, the two national parties gather to nominate candidates for the presidency and minor party or independent candidates are completing the state-by-state process of gaining access to the general election ballot. The candidates then present themselves to a national electorate at a single election, and the winner has the unique responsibility of representing all Americans.

Table 2-1   The Growth of Presidential Primaries, 1968–1992

	Democratic Party			Republican Party			
Year	Number of primaries	Votes cast	Delegates selected through primaries (in percent)	Number of primaries	Votes cast	Delegates selected through primaries (in percent)	Total delegates selected through primaries (in percent)
1968	15	7,535,069	40.2	15	4,473,551	38.1	39.1
1972	21	15,993,965	65.3	20	6,188,281	56.8	61.0
1976	27	16,052,652	76.0	26	10,374,125	71.0	73.5
1980	35	18,747,825	71.8	35	12,690,451	76.0	73.7
1984	30	18,009,217	52.4	25	6,575,651	71.0	59.6
1988	37	22,961,936	66.6	37	12,165,115	76.9	70.2
1992	40	20,239,385	66.9	39	12,696,547	83.9	72.7

Sources: Congressional Quarterly's Guide to the Presidency, ed. Michael Nelson (Washington, D.C.: Congressional Quarterly Inc., 1989); and *America Votes* 20, ed. Richard M. Scammon and Alice C. McGillivray (Washington, D.C.: Congressional Quarterly Inc., 1993).

Table 2-2 Federal Matching Funds to 1992 Presidential Candidates

Candidates	Federal matching funds
Democrats	
Larry Agran	$ 269,691
Jerry Brown	4,239,345
Bill Clinton	12,518,130
Tom Harkin	2,103,352
Bob Kerrey	2,198,284
Lyndon LaRouche	568,434
Paul Tsongas	3,039,388
Doug Wilder	289,026
Total Democrats	25,225,650
Republicans	
Patrick Buchanan	4,999,983
George Bush	10,658,513
Total Republicans	15,658,496
Other party	
Lenora Fulani	1,935,524
John Hagelin	353,160
Total Other Party	2,288,684
Grand Total	43,172,830

Source: Federal Election Commission.

Note: Data covers the time period from January 1, 1991, through December 31, 1994.

Table 2-3 Early Starts in the Presidential Campaign

Election year	Major declared candidates announcing before June 30 of year preceding election	
	Number	Percentage
1968	0	0
1972	1	7
1976	6	43
1980	5	50
1984	6	67
1988	10	71
1992	1	11
1996	9	NA

Note: NA = Not Available.

Table 2-4   Precampaign Vehicles of Declared 1996 Presidential Candidates, as of
June 1995

Candidate	PAC	Foundation
Lamar Alexander	Republican Fund for the '90s	
Pat Buchanan		The American Cause
Robert Dole	Campaign America	Better America Foundation
Robert Dornan	American Citizens for Political Action	
	American Space Frontier Committee	
Phil Gramm	Leadership for America	
Alan Keyes	Campaign for Maryland's Future	
Richard Lugar	Republican Senate Majority Fund	
Arlen Specter	Big Tent PAC	

Notes: Declared candidates as of August 1995; Pete Wilson and Morry Taylor did not have organizations that served as precampaign vehicles.

Table 2-5   The Changing Democratic Party Rules: Delegate Allocation Schemes, 1984–1996

	Delegates selected			
Delegate allocation rule	1984	1988	1992	1996
Proportional representation	37%	42%	71%	71%
Bonus	17	20	[a]	[a]
Loophole	24	12	[a]	[a]
Pledged party and elected officials	8	11	11	11
Unpledged	14	16	18	18

Source: Democratic National Committee.

Note: Bonus = proportional representation plus winner-take-more; loophole = winner-take-all; pledged party and elected officials = allocated proportional representation at-large.

[a] Abolished.

Table 2-6 1996 Democratic Delegate Selection Calendar: Primaries and Caucuses

Date	State	Apportionment method	Total delegate votes
February 12	Iowa	Caucus	56
February 20	New Hampshire	Primary	26
February 24	Delaware	Primary	21
February 24–26	Democrats abroad	Caucus	9
February 27	South Dakota	Primary	23
February 29–March 14	North Dakota	Caucus	22
March 5	American Samoa	Caucus	6
	Colorado	Primary	58
	Connecticut	Primary	65
	Georgia	Primary	91
	Idaho	Caucus	24
	Maine	Primary	32
	Maryland	Primary	85
	Massachusetts	Primary	114
	Minnesota	Caucus	92
	Rhode Island	Primary	31
	South Carolina	Caucus	52
	Vermont	Primary	22
	Washington	Caucus	91
March 7	New York	Primary	288
	Missouri	Caucus	92
March 9	Alaska	Caucus	19
	Arizona	Primary	52
March 10	Nevada	Caucus	27
	Puerto Rico	Primary	58
March 12	Florida	Primary	177
	Hawaii	Caucus	30
	Louisiana	Primary	75
	Mississippi	Primary	49
	Oklahoma	Primary	53
	Oregon	Primary	56
	Tennessee	Primary	83
	Texas	Caucus and primary	230
March 16	Michigan	Primary	158
March 19	Illinois	Primary	194
	Ohio	Primary	171
	Wisconsin	Primary	93
March 23	Wyoming	Caucus	19
March 25	Utah	Caucus	30
March 26	California	Primary	423
March 30	Virgin Islands	Caucus	4
April 2	Kansas	Primary	41
April 13	Virginia	Caucus	96
April 23	Pennsylvania	Primary	195
May 5	Guam	Caucus	6
May 7	District of Columbia	Primary	38
	Indiana	Primary	89
	North Carolina	Primary	98
May 14	Nebraska	Primary	33
	West Virginia	Primary	42
May 21	Arkansas	Primary	48
May 28	Kentucky	Primary	61

Continued on next page

Table 2-6   *Continued*

Date	State	Apportionment method	Total delegate votes
June 4	Alabama	Primary	66
	Montana	Primary	25
	New Jersey	Primary	120
	New Mexico	Primary	34

Source: Democratic National Committee and *Congressional Quarterly Weekly Report,* August 19, 1995.

Note: Dates listed are for primaries or first-round caucuses in which presidential candidates are allotted convention delegates on the basis of primary or caucus votes. Nonbinding or "beauty contest" primaries are excluded. In some cases, the actual selection of individuals to be delegates may occur later or through a completely distinct process on a different schedule. "Total delegate votes" includes both those delegates apportioned through the primary or caucus process and unpledged delegate votes or "superdelegates." Primary and caucus dates and method of selection are those in effect on August 15, 1995. The Democratic National Convention will be held August 26–29, 1996.

Table 2-7   1996 Republican Delegate Selection Calendar: Primaries and Caucuses

Date	State	Apportionment method	Total delegate votes
January 25–31	Hawaii	Caucus	14
January 26–29	Alaska	Caucus	19
February 6	Louisiana	Caucus	28
February 12	Iowa	Caucus	25
February 20	New Hampshire	Primary	16
February 24	Delaware	Primary	12
February 27	Arizona	Primary	39
	North Dakota	Primary	18
	South Dakota	Primary	18
March	Nevada	Caucus	14
	Wyoming	Caucus	20
March 2	South Carolina	Primary	37
March 3	Puerto Rico	Primary	14
	Virgin Islands	Caucus	4
March 5	American Samoa	Caucus	4
	Colorado	Primary	27
	Connecticut	Primary	27
	Georgia	Primary	42
	Maine	Primary	15
	Maryland	Primary	32
	Massachusetts	Primary	37
	Minnesota	Caucus	33
	Rhode Island	Primary	16
	Vermont	Primary	12
	Washington	Caucus	36
March 7	New York	Primary	102
March 9	Missouri	Caucus	36
March 12	Florida	Primary	98
	Louisiana	Primary	28
	Mississippi	Primary	32
	Oklahoma	Primary	38
	Oregon	Primary	23
	Tennessee	Primary	37
	Texas	Primary	123

Table 2-7   *Continued*

Date	State	Apportionment method	Total delegate votes
March 17	Puerto Rico	Primary	14
March 19	Illinois	Primary	69
	Michigan	Primary	57
	Ohio	Primary	67
	Wisconsin	Primary	36
March 25	Utah	Caucus	28
March 26	California	Primary	163
April 2	Kansas	Primary	31
April 23	Pennsylvania	Primary	73
May 7	District of Columbia	Primary	14
	Indiana	Primary	52
	North Carolina	Primary	58
May 14	Nebraska	Primary	24
	West Virginia	Primary	18
May 21	Arkansas	Primary	20
May 28	Idaho	Primary	23
	Kentucky	Primary	26
June 4	Alabama	Primary	40
	Montana	Primary	14
	New Jersey	Primary	48
	New Mexico	Primary	18

Source: Republican National Committee and *Congressional Quarterly Weekly Report,* August 19, 1995.

Note: Dates listed are for primaries or first-round caucuses in which presidential candidates are allotted convention delegate votes on the basis of primary or caucus balloting. In Louisiana both a caucus and primary that allocate convention delegates are held; therefore the state is listed twice. Nonbinding or "beauty contest" primaries are excluded. The actual selection of individuals to be delegates may occur later or through a completely distinct process on a different schedule. "Total delegate votes" includes both delegates apportioned through the primary or caucus process and others who may be appointed by state party leadership irrespective of primary or caucus results. Primary and caucus dates and method of selection are those in effect on August 15, 1995. At that time, Republicans in Virginia had not yet selected a date for their primary or caucus. The Republican National Convention will be held August 10–16, 1996.

Exercises

1. You are a citizen in the state of New Columbia, which sends twenty delegates to the convention. Today the presidential primary election takes place. Assuming that your classmates are fellow citizens of New Columbia, conduct a primary with the following rule:

• The presidential candidate who receives the most votes receives all twenty delegates.

Hold the election a second time, with each student voting for the same candidate as in the first election. However, for the second election use the following rules:

• The class is divided into four equal groups.

• The presidential candidate who receives the most votes in each group receives four delegates.

• The presidential candidate who receives the most votes in each group receives one bonus delegate.

Hold the election a third time, with students again voting for the same candidate. However, for this election use the following rules:

• The class is divided into four equal groups.

• In each group, all candidates receiving 15 percent or more of the vote are allotted one to four delegates based on their share of the vote. Candidates receiving less than 15 percent of the vote win no delegates.

Compare the results of each election in terms of delegate allocation. Which seems the fairest? Which is the most "representative" of the electorate?

2. In 1996 the majority of delegates to the major party nominating conventions were chosen in the shortest time period ever (see Tables 2-6 and 2-7). Is this good or bad for the presidential selection process? Explain.

3. Select a state and analyze the Democratic or Republican caucus or primary results. Using biographical information on the candidates contained in the candidate profiles section, compare the characteristics of the candidates with the political and demographic profile of the chosen state. What might explain the primary or caucus results?

4. Select one Republican candidate and analyze his or her strategy prior to the selection of delegates for the 1996 convention. How did this candidate communicate first with core supporters and later with the broader public? What precampaign vehicles did the candidate use for his or her declaration of candidacy (see Table 2-4)?

5. Focusing on one of the media debates among the candidates, compare your assessment of the debate with the "morning after" press evaluation. How did the press determine winners and losers? How does the press assessment compare with your own?

6. In the 1992 campaign, media exposés of Gov. Bill Clinton's personal life played a critical role in the campaign preliminaries. In the early stages of the 1996 campaign, media coverage also has focused on comparable dimensions of the private lives of declared or potential candidates.

Is this type of reporting appropriate for the media? Does the public have the right to know all personal information related to a candidate? If not, what kinds of information should be reported and what should not?

7. "How much money is necessary?" was one of the critical questions related to the Republican nomination in 1996. What was the role of money in the Republican race for the nomination?

8. Many of the recent changes in the Democratic rules for selecting delegates have been rationalized on the basis of producing a more "representative" convention. Review the changes in these rules over the last two decades (see Table 2-5), identifying which rules produce representative conventions and which do not. What would be the ideal set of rules for achieving a representative convention?

9. The Republican and Democratic parties have different rules and philosophies regarding the selection of delegates to their national nominating conventions. Compare these rules and philosophies, analyzing their impact upon each party. For example, have the Democratic rules produced more representative conventions but more losing candidates?

10. Review the precise circumstances surrounding the withdrawal of candidates from the 1996 presidential campaign. List the characteristics of each situation and try to determine the role of money, caucus or primary results, adverse publicity, and other factors in ending the campaigns.

11. Critics charge that only a select and unrepresentative sample of party members participate in delegate selection caucuses while a broader and more representative sample of party members participates in primaries. Is the primary system then better than the caucus system? Do alternative methods exist that might be preferable?

12. Identify and evaluate the procedures for third parties or independent candidates to secure nomination for the general election ballot in your state.

Additional Sources
Printed Material and Videos

"Ballot Access News." A newsletter focusing on state laws and judicial decisions that affect the access of minor parties and independent candidates to the ballot. Published by the Coalition for Free and Open Elections, this is an invaluable source of information about state-by-state election and ballot regulations.

Corrado, Anthony. *Paying for Presidents*. New York: Twentieth Century Fund, 1993. An insightful review of the interaction of federal campaign finance laws with the presidential selection process. One chapter focuses specifically on financing primary campaigns.

"Democratic Urban Precinct Caucus." A video of one of the 1988 Iowa precinct caucuses showing the unique bargaining that is possible between supporters for different candidates. Available from the Purdue University Public Affairs Video Archives.

"Media Monitor." A newsletter that focuses on the national media's treatment of social and political issues. Published by the Center for Media and Public Affairs. Several issues in late 1991 and early 1992 dealt with media coverage of the 1992 campaign.

On-Line Data

"CNN Interactive." This is Cable News Network's on-line news service featuring both text and audio segments related to the top political stories of the day. The site includes links to numerous other sites focusing on the 1996 presidential selection process as it unfolds.
Access method: World Wide Web
To access: http://www.cnn.com/
Choose: Politics

"Election '96." This is the most comprehensive on-line directory of links to 1996 election data, grouped by parties and candidates, issues, and other election-related stories. This page also hosts an all-candidate, all-party straw poll.
Access method: World Wide Web
To access: http://dodo.crown.net/~mpg/election/96.html
Choose: Almost all options provide information relevant to the election

"Iowa CyberCaucus." This source offers a comprehensive look at Iowa's caucus system through its history and by party. It also provides ongoing 1996 Iowa caucus news.
Access method: World Wide Web
To access: http://www.drake.edu/public/news.html
Choose: All options are relevant to the topic

"NH-Primary." This site is dedicated to the New Hampshire primary. It has a research archive for each candidate and campaign, New Hampshire primary news, local polling data, and a moderated discussion list for the primary campaign.
Access method: World Wide Web
To access: http://unhinfo.unh.edu/unh/acad/libarts/comm/nhprimary/nhprim.html
Choose: All options are relevant to the topic

"The Gallup Organization." This is the on-line site of one of the nation's largest and most prestigious pollsters; it includes a review of recent issues of Gallup's monthly magazine, which contains data on candidate standings in the polls.
Access method: World Wide Web
To access: http://www.gallup.com/
Choose: Gallup Poll Monthly Newsletter Archives

Nominees Bill Clinton and Al Gore celebrate their victory at the Democratic National Convention, New York City, July 16, 1992.

3

Nomination

Although not all presidential candidates are formally nominated by conventions, the major party nominating conventions continue to be important to all nominees. Clearly, major party nominees rely upon these gatherings for both their nominations and the fashioning of a coalition of party members to support their candidacies. Despite declining major party loyalties, the viability of third-party or independent candidacies also remains closely tied to the dynamics of the major party conventions.

At a significant number of major party conventions in the last forty years, one clear choice for the nomination was accepted by virtually all segments of the party. This individual faced little or no opposition prior to the convention and was nominated on the first ballot. Franklin D. Roosevelt in 1936 and 1944, Dwight D. Eisenhower in 1956, Lyndon B. Johnson in 1964, Richard Nixon in 1972, and Ronald Reagan in 1984 are examples of such a candidate (see Tables 3-1, 3-2, and 3-3). In these cases, the other functions of the national nominating convention, such as the fashioning of a party platform and the accreditation of delegates, are generally performed with ease and a minimum of controversy. This unanimity has also narrowed the electoral opportunities for third parties or independent candidates.

Participants at major party conventions characterized by consensus, however, may squabble over matters that relate to future nom-inees. Given that most of these conventions are nominating incumbent presidents for a second term, an unavoidable consideration is who will emerge as the heir apparent to the current chief executive. For example, at the 1956 and 1972 Republican conventions, the only matters of dispute related to the vice presidential nomination and the formula for allocating delegates for the next Republican convention. Clearly, each of these squabbles was the opening round for the 1960 and 1976 Republican nominations, respectively.

At the other extreme are major party conventions at which presidential nominations are made only after intense ideological or factional conflict. In these cases, the nomination is hotly contested throughout the caucuses and primaries and occasionally (although not since 1952) resolved only after multiple convention ballots. Conflict pervades virtually every aspect of these conventions. These situations are made especially difficult when partisans in the struggles place more emphasis on their commitment to particular policy stands or to a particular candidate than on the nomination of a party standard-bearer who can win in November. One clear consequence of major party conventions with a significant level of unresolved conflict is that they increase the opportunities for third-party or independent candidates by prompting disgruntled major party members to support such candidacies.

Despite damaging public displays of rancor and intraparty discord at past major party conventions, these were nonetheless part of a presidential selection process rooted in a stable two-party system in which major party dissidents had a short life as independents or third-party members. Within one election cycle, for example, most supporters of Henry Wallace's third-party campaign in 1948, George Wallace's independent campaign in 1968, or John Anderson's independent campaign in 1980 had been reintegrated into a two-party system.

In a fundamentally new presidential selection process in which old political labels are less meaningful, public identification with parties is declining, and political movements based on compelling personalities are on the rise, however, national nominating conventions become even more difficult excercises in brokering major party coalitions. To a very large degree, this is the case because the major parties themselves are now less at the center of the nominating process than at any time since conventions first developed in the early nineteenth century. The fact that convention proceedings are now conveyed to a more independent-minded public through selective media coverage makes their successful operation only more difficult.

1996 Considerations

For both major parties, the 1996 nominating conventions present great peril. A successful convention will not only depend upon the parties brokering or resolving intraparty differences in a period of great political and ideological flux but also sending a clear and consistent message through the media as to who they are and what they represent.

The overall goal for President Clinton within the electoral arithmetic of a two-way presidential race is to fashion a coalition of liberal and moderate Democrats who enthusiastically support his renomination. In a three- or even four-way presidential election, which would most likely be apparent by the time of the Democratic convention in August, the electoral arithmetic would be quite different. Indeed, the president could potentially be reelected with even less than the 43 percent of the total vote he received in 1992. In this scenario, the president would attempt to appeal to a narrower segment of voters, either in the middle or on the left of the political spectrum, and the general themes of the convention would reflect this strategy. An additional challenge for the president is gaining full support of the legislative wing of the Democratic Party, devastated in the 1994 midterm elections. The possibility of further losses makes congressional Democrats wary electoral partners for the president.

The challenge for Republicans is no less great. In 1992 Republicans were perceived by many voters as harsh, exclusionary, and out of the political mainstream. These perceptions obviously undercut the ability of President Bush's reelection campaign to gain any sustained postconvention momentum. In 1996 Republicans face a similar risk. The increasing power of the religious right within the Republican Party, and the ability of more strident candidates such as Pat Buchanan to set the tone of the early campaign, threaten similar portrayals of the 1996 Republican convention. The entry of Speaker of the House Newt Gingrich, R- Ga., into the Republican campaign would further compound this potential problem by riveting the eager media to one of the most well-known, controversial, and enigmatic politicians.

The 1992 major party conventions reinforced how critical a role the media play. In the midst of what was considered to be a successful Democratic convention, candidate Clinton received, according to the Center for Media and Public Affairs, 68 percent positive evaluations from stories that appeared on network evening news shows. At a Republican convention roundly condemned to be out of the political mainstream, President Bush received only 49 percent positive evaluations.

It is no surprise, then, that the major parties spend considerable energy attempting to ensure that their conventions will receive both wide and positive media coverage. These efforts include adjusting the convention schedule to network programming demands, distributing of sound bites, providing video footage, and allowing live convention programming. At the 1992 Democratic convention, for example, local and independent stations were able to interview party officials on the convention floor or in studios set up in Madison Square Garden. These interviews were then beamed via the convention's Satellite News Service to local news bureaus. Republicans also arranged interviews for small- to medium-market television stations via their own satellite technology at the 1992 Republican convention while additionally assembling daily video news releases for distribution to these stations. In sum, contemporary conventions pit party leaders attempting to control the public image of the proceedings against thousands of journalists who descend upon the convention searching for "news."

Points of Concern

Despite the importance of a positive public image of convention proceedings, conflict may appear at several critical points. First, if the nomination remains in doubt at the start of the convention, disputes over the basic rules that govern the proceedings and that can have a direct impact upon the presidential nomination are possible. These rules deal with matters such as the length of debate on the convention floor, whether delegates can vote on issues directly affecting their own status at the convention, and whether presidential aspirants must announce a running mate before the balloting for president. At the 1980 Democratic convention, supporters of Massachusetts senator Edward M. Kennedy proposed that the rule requiring delegates to vote for the candidate to whom they were pledged be abolished (see Table 3-4). The change would have aided Kennedy, who was trailing President Jimmy Carter in pledged delegates.

Second, at closely contested conventions, the accreditation of particular delegates may become an issue. For example, the challenge to the seating of certain delegates at the 1968 Democratic convention was closely related to the efforts of supporters of Sens. Eugene J. McCarthy of Minnesota and George McGovern of South Dakota to prevent the nomination of Vice President Hubert H. Humphrey. Similarly, the challenge to the seating of some delegates at the 1972 Democratic convention was related to tactical maneuvering by both pro- and anti-McGovern forces.

Third, when conventions are divided among factional and ideological rivals, the approval of a platform poses another potentially volatile scene. Some intraparty differences over rival presidential aspirants represent deep divisions within the party over issues. In 1964, for example, the split within the Republican Party between supporters of Sen. Barry M. Goldwater of Arizona and anti-Goldwater forces was reflected early in the convention by a key vote over the platform plank on civil rights. In 1968 the split between Humphrey and anti-Humphrey forces at the Democratic convention mirrored differences regarding American policy in Vietnam. In this respect, the convention vote on the Vietnam plank of the platform also was essentially a warm-up vote for the presidential nomination.

Finally, the nomination of a vice presidential candidate may reveal unresolved factional or ideological battles within the party. Since 1940, when Franklin D. Roosevelt handpicked his vice president, nominees for president have controlled the vice presidential nominating process, selecting running mates with whom they feel both personally and ideologically comfortable. The nomination for vice president, however, provides the opportunity for losing or disgruntled factions within the party to pursue at least some of their unfulfilled goals. While vice presidential nominations of this sort generally are not much more than symbolic efforts, they can signal that the party has yet to achieve broad support for the presidential nominee or for the platform.

At best, a vice presidential nominee may soothe factional differences within the party, avert controversy, and ultimately aid the ticket in winning his or her home state. A significant number of recent vice presidential nominees have failed to meet these far from rigorous requirements. In 1972 the Democratic candidate for vice president was forced to resign within two weeks of his nomination, following revelations that he had been hospitalized three times for "nervous exhaustion and fatigue." In 1984 and 1988 Democratic and Republican vice presidential nominees faced allegations of ethical improprieties. In 1992 Vice President Quayle's support in public opinion polls was so low that President Bush seriously considered replacing him.

The major party national nominating conventions, therefore, reflect both a struggle for power within the party and an attempt to maintain, if not solidify, the coalitions that comprise the party. Balancing these two goals is a difficult task made even more sensitive because it occurs in public, under the watchful eyes of thousands of journalists. This situation is fraught with danger for the party and the nominee. As former Democratic National Committee chairman Robert Strauss put it, conventions "are made for mischief."

Major Party Conventions: Media Events

Before a convention convenes, many of its basic features have been established by the committees of the convention. For both parties these committees deal with the establishment of rules governing the convention, the acceptance of credentials of the convention delegates, the development of a party platform, and a myriad of specific arrangements for the convention. Prior to the presentation of the recommendations of these committees, however, the convention has other business to perform. Initial convention events generally include welcoming speeches by officials from the host city and state, election of convention officers, reports

from national party officials, speeches by party notables, and the convention keynote address.

The keynote address is especially important because it sets the general tone of the convention, stressing the party's chosen themes, and provides national exposure for the individual giving the address. Such exposure may further a well-developed national career or, indeed, may suddenly create one. For example, at the 1976 Democratic convention, keynoter Barbara Jordan received votes for both president and vice president—apparently the result of her dramatic address.

In a period of selective coverage by the television networks (no network aired more than two hours of convention proceedings per day in 1992, while all three networks provided gavel-to-gavel coverage before 1976), only prime-time convention events reach national audiences. As a result, some changes in the structure of conventions have occurred, with the parties scheduling during the day potentially divisive proceedings, mundane party business, and controversial speakers who cannot be denied the podium. Select party notables and the nominees appear during the one or two hours of nightly network coverage. Although the keynote address has maintained its traditional importance as one of these critical presentations, other prime-time speeches by party officials or notables can now have an equally defining national impact. In 1992, for example, several prime-time addresses at the Republican convention, including those by Patrick Buchanan and Marilyn Quayle, wife of the vice president, created a negative public image of the Republican convention and conveyed a strident tone, even though dozens of non-prime-time speeches reflected a more low-keyed orientation.

Before the nomination of candidates, the convention generally reviews reports on party rules, acceptance of delegate credentials, and the party platform. Although the convention committees and the national party committees attempt to achieve consensus or compromise in all of these areas before the convention convenes, that is not always possible. When a minimum number delegate signatures are secured (20 percent of the appropriate convention committee for the Democrats; 25 percent for the Republicans), both a majority report and minority positions are presented to the convention—a situation that can provide great drama for the mass media and give the impression of significant intraparty conflict to the public. Parties and prospective nominees therefore make great efforts to avoid or minimize such situations. In 1984, 1988, and 1992 the apparent Democratic nominees made a wide range of concessions to their vanquished opponents in order to avoid major floor fights at the upcoming conventions. According to Walter Mondale's aide, Tom Donilon, these agreements were crucial because "[t]he floor will be clear to do what we want to do on television."

Finally the convention turns to what many view as its business—the nomination of presidential and vice presidential candidates. Decisions about rules or credentials already may have determined the outcome of the nominating process, but the convention nonetheless moves through a ritual as old as the convention itself.

Candidates who have the required minimal number of delegate signatures (three hundred with no more than fifty from any one state for the Democrats; the majority of delegates from five states for the Republicans) are placed in nomination by prominent supporters, and a "spontaneous" demonstration of support ensues. With the advent of television and the nominee's desire to address the greatest number of viewers possible, these spontaneous demonstrations have been curtailed. When convention events are not controlled, unfortunate consequences can result. For example, in 1972 Democratic nominee McGovern finally took the podium to give his acceptance speech at 2:48 a.m., far past prime-time television viewing.

Eventually the convention votes for the nominees on a state-by-state basis. In a close contest, the voting process itself can generate considerable suspense. States may not vote when called or they may stop the state-by-state polling process because they are completing their tally. Additionally, when the result of the polling is obvious after all states have voted or had the opportunity to vote, some states may change their votes. (This change is technically labeled a "shift.") The goal is to be part of the winning coalition.

The convention then moves to balloting for the vice presidential nomination. The presidential nominee selects the vice presidential nominee, who is virtually assured of receiving the nomination by a voting majority of delegates or by acclamation. However, exceptions to this rule exist. In 1956 Democratic nominee Adlai Stevenson decided to leave the choice to the convention. In the chaotic balloting that followed, a relatively unknown Massachusetts senator, John F. Kennedy, came just forty votes short of the vice presidential nomination.

The culmination of modern media conventions is the acceptance speeches of the presidential and vice presidential nominees. Nominees did not appear before the convention before 1932, when Franklin D. Roosevelt accepted the nomination in person, establishing the tradition among Democrats. Republican nominee Wendell Willkie began this practice among Republicans in 1940.

Just as prime-time speeches by party notables set the tone for the convention, the acceptance speech sets the tone for the upcoming campaign. Barry Goldwater, in accepting the 1964 Republican nomination, uttered perhaps the most prominent statement of the entire campaign: "And let me remind you that extremism in the defense of liberty is no vice. And let me remind you also that moderation in the pursuit of justice is no virtue."

In an age where increasingly sophisticated communications technology has made images and sounds as important as words, acceptance speeches also become multidimensional presentations of the candidate to one of the largest audiences of the campaign. Whether the nominee can successfully communicate in this fashion is the first great test of his or her candidacy.

In 1992 the Democrats mastered this challenge by concluding Clinton's acceptance speech with perhaps the convention's most telegenic moment: the presidential and vice presidential candidates dancing with their wives to Fleetwood Mac's "Don't Stop (Thinking About Tomorrow)."

After the acceptance speeches, the convention adjourns to prepare for the upcoming campaign. Although campaigns have traditionally not begun until Labor Day, the conventions and the impressions they have left upon the public have already set much of the groundwork for either success or failure in November. In 1992 Democrats altered this long-established schedule by sending their nominees on two-week bus tours throughout eleven states immediately after the highly successful convention.

Table 3-1 Democratic Conventions, 1832–1992

Year	Location	Presidential nominee	Ballots
1832	Baltimore, Md.	Andrew Jackson	1
1835	Baltimore, Md.	Martin Van Buren	1
1840	Baltimore, Md.	Martin Van Buren	1
1844	Baltimore, Md.	James K. Polk	9
1848	Baltimore, Md.	Lewis Cass	4
1852	Baltimore, Md.	Franklin Pierce	49
1856	Cincinnati, Ohio	James Buchanan	17
1860	Charleston, S.C.	Deadlocked	57
	Baltimore, Md.	Stephen A. Douglas	2
1864	Chicago, Ill.	George B. McClellan	1
1868	New York, N.Y.	Horatio Seymour	22
1872	Baltimore, Md.	Horace Greeley	1
1876	St. Louis, Mo.	Samuel J. Tilden	2
1880	Cincinnati, Ohio	Winfield S. Hancock	2
1884	Chicago, Ill.	Grover Cleveland	2
1888	St. Louis, Mo.	Grover Cleveland	1
1892	Chicago, Ill.	Grover Cleveland	1
1896	Chicago, Ill.	William J. Bryan	5
1900	Kansas City, Mo.	William J. Bryan	1
1904	St. Louis, Mo.	Alton S. Parker	1
1908	Denver, Colo.	William J. Bryan	1
1912	Baltimore, Md.	Woodrow Wilson	46
1916	St. Louis, Mo.	Woodrow Wilson	1
1920	San Francisco, Calif.	James M. Cox	44
1924	New York, N.Y.	John W. Davis	103
1928	Houston, Texas	Alfred E. Smith	1
1932	Chicago, Ill.	Franklin D. Roosevelt	4
1936	Philadelphia, Pa.	Franklin D. Roosevelt	Acclamation
1940	Chicago, Ill.	Franklin D. Roosevelt	1
1944	Chicago, Ill.	Franklin D. Roosevelt	1
1948	Philadelphia, Pa.	Harry S. Truman	1
1952	Chicago, Ill.	Adlai E. Stevenson	3
1956	Chicago, Ill.	Adlai E. Stevenson	1
1960	Los Angeles, Calif.	John F. Kennedy	1
1964	Atlantic City, N.J.	Lyndon B. Johnson	Acclamation
1968	Chicago, Ill.	Hubert H. Humphrey	1
1972	Miami Beach, Fla.	George McGovern	1
1976	New York, N.Y.	Jimmy Carter	1
1980	New York, N.Y.	Jimmy Carter	1

Table 3-1 *Continued*

Year	Location	Presidential nominee	Ballots
1984	San Francisco, Calif.	Walter F. Mondale	1
1988	Atlanta, Ga.	Michael S. Dukakis	1
1992	New York, N.Y.	Bill Clinton	1

Source: National Party Conventions 1831–1992 (Washington, D.C.: Congressional Quarterly Inc., 1995), 10.

Table 3-2 Republican Conventions, 1856–1992

Year	Location	Presidential nominee	Ballots
1856	Philadelphia, Pa.	John C. Fremont	2
1860	Chicago, Ill.	Abraham Lincoln	3
1864	Baltimore, Md.	Abraham Lincoln	1
1868	Chicago, Ill.	Ulysses S. Grant	1
1872	Philadelphia, Pa.	Ulysses S. Grant	1
1876	Cincinnati, Ohio	Rutherford B. Hayes	7
1880	Chicago, Ill.	James A. Garfield	36
1884	Chicago, Ill.	James G. Blaine	4
1888	Chicago, Ill.	Benjamin Harrison	8
1892	Minneapolis, Minn.	Benjamin Harrison	1
1896	St. Louis, Mo.	William McKinley	1
1900	Philadelphia, Pa.	William McKinley	1
1904	Chicago, Ill.	Theodore Roosevelt	1
1908	Chicago, Ill.	William H. Taft	1
1912	Chicago, Ill.	William H. Taft	1
1916	Chicago, Ill.	Charles E. Hughes	3
1920	Chicago, Ill.	Warren G. Harding	10
1924	Cleveland, Ohio	Calvin Coolidge	1
1928	Kansas City, Mo.	Herbert Hoover	1
1932	Chicago, Ill.	Herbert Hoover	1
1936	Cleveland, Ohio	Alfred M. Landon	1
1940	Philadelphia, Pa.	Wendell Willkie	6
1944	Chicago, Ill.	Thomas E. Dewey	1
1948	Philadelphia, Pa.	Thomas E. Dewey	3
1952	Chicago, Ill.	Dwight D. Eisenhower	1
1956	San Francisco, Calif.	Dwight D. Eisenhower	1
1960	Chicago, Ill.	Richard Nixon	1
1964	San Francisco, Calif.	Barry M. Goldwater	1
1968	Miami Beach, Fla.	Richard Nixon	1
1972	Miami Beach, Fla.	Richard Nixon	1
1976	Kansas City, Mo.	Gerald R. Ford	1
1980	Detroit, Mich.	Ronald Reagan	1
1984	Dallas, Texas	Ronald Reagan	1
1988	New Orleans, La.	George Bush	1
1992	Houston, Texas	George Bush	1

Source: National Party Conventions, 1831–1992 (Washington, D.C.: Congressional Quarterly Inc., 1995), 12.

Table 3-3 First-Ballot Voting for Presidential Nominees at Democratic and Republican Conventions, 1972–1992

Convention	Votes needed to nominate	Presidential nominee	Votes received[a]
1972 Democratic	1,509	George McGovern	1,728
		Henry M. Jackson	525
		George C. Wallace	382
		Shirley Chisholm	152
		Terry Sanford	78
1972 Republican	675	Richard Nixon	1,347
		Pete McCloskey	1
1976 Democratic	1,505	Jimmy Carter	2,239
		Morris K. Udall	330
		Edmund G. Brown, Jr.	301
		George C. Wallace	57
1976 Republican	1,130	Gerald R. Ford	1,187
		Ronald Reagan	1,070
1980 Democratic	1,666	Jimmy Carter	2,123
		Edward M. Kennedy	1,150
1980 Republican	998	Ronald Reagan	1,939
		John B. Anderson	37
		George Bush	13
1984 Democratic	1,967	Walter F. Mondale	2,191
		Gary Hart	1,201
		Jesse Jackson	466
1984 Republican	1,118	Ronald Reagan	2,233
1988 Democratic	2,082	Michael S. Dukakis	2,876
		Jesse Jackson	1,219
1988 Republican	1,140	George Bush	2,277
1992 Democratic	2,145	Bill Clinton	3,372
		Edmund G. Brown, Jr.	596
		Paul Tsongas	209
1992 Republican	1,106	George Bush	2,166
		Patrick Buchanan	18

Source: National Party Conventions, 1831–1992 (Washington, D.C.: Congressional Quarterly Inc., 1995), 234–248.

[a] Fractional votes rounded to nearest whole number.

Table 3-4 Prominent Rules, Credentials, and Platform Disputes at the National Convention, 1924–1992

Convention	Issue	Vote[a]
1924 Democratic	Formal opposition of the Democratic Party to the Ku Klux Klan	Yea, 542; nay, 543
1932 Republican	Repeal of prohibition	Yea, 460; nay, 691
1948 Democratic	Amendment to platform statement on civil rights to include commendation of President Truman's civil rights program and support for congressional action in civil rights	Yea, 652; nay, 583

Table 3-4 *Continued*

Convention	Issue	Vote[a]
1952 Democratic	Seating of Virginia delegation despite its refusal to abide by earlier convention resolution requiring all delegates to work to place the national Democratic Party ticket on the ballot under the party's name in their state	Yea, 651; nay, 518
1964 Republican	Amendment to platform statement on civil rights to include specific pledges of speedy school desegregation, full voting rights, and the elimination of job discrimination	Yea, 409; nay, 897
1968 Democratic	Abolition of the unit rule	Yea, 1,351; nay, 1,209
1968 Democratic	Amendment to platform statement on Vietnam to include a call for the immediate halt of the bombing of North Vietnam, reduction of offensive operations in South Vietnam, a negotiated troop withdrawal, and establishment of a coalition government in South Vietnam	Yea, 1,041; nay, 1,568
1972 Democratic	Seating of the California delegation despite its election by winner-take-all primary that was in violation of party rules	Yea, 1,618; nay, 1,238
1976 Republican	Requirement that all presidential candidates name their running mates prior to the convention vote for president	Yea, 1,069; nay, 1,180
1980 Democratic	Abolition of party rule binding delegates for one ballot to vote for candidates to whom they were pledged	Yea, 1,391; nay, 1,936
1984 Democratic	Abolition of dual primaries	Yea, 1,253; nay, 2,501
1988 Democratic	Amendment to platform pledging that the United States would make "no first use" of nuclear weapons	Yea, 1,221; nay, 2,474
1992 Democratic	Amendment to platform to delay a middle-class tax cut and a tax credit for families and children until the deficit was under control	Yea, 953; nay, 2,287

Source: National Party Conventions, 1831–1992 (Washington, D.C.: Congressional Quarterly Inc., 1995).

[a] Franctional votes rounded to nearest whole number

Table 3-5 Votes for African American Candidates at Major Party Conventions

Convention	Candidate	Office	Votes received[a]
1880 Republican	Blanche K. Bruce	Vice president	8
1888 Republican	Frederick Douglass	President	1
	Blanche K. Bruce	Vice president	11
1968 Democratic	Channing E. Phillips	President	68
	Julian Bond	Vice president	49
1968 Republican	Edward W. Brooke	Vice president	1
1972 Democratic	Shirley Chisholm	President	152

Continued on next page

Table 3-5 *Continued*

Convention	Candidate	Office	Votes received[a]
	Shirley Chisholm	Vice president	20
1976 Democratic	Barbara Jordan	President	1
	Ronald V. Dellums	Vice president	20
	Barbara Jordan	Vice president	28
1980 Democratic	Ronald V. Dellums	President	3
1984 Democratic	Jesse Jackson	President	466
	Shirley Chisholm	Vice president	39
1988 Democratic	Jesse Jackson	President	1,219
1992 Republican	Alan Keyes	President	1

Sources: Richard C. Bain and Judith H. Parris, *Convention Decisions and Voting Records* (Washington, D.C.: The Brookings Institution, 1973); *National Party Conventions, 1831–1992* (Washington, D.C.: Congressional Quarterly Inc., 1995); and official proceedings of the Democratic and Republican conventions, 1880–1992.

[a] Fractional votes rounded to nearest whole number.

Table 3–6 Votes for Women Candidates at Major Party Conventions

Convention	Candidate	Office	Votes received[a]
1920 Democratic	Laura Clay	President	1
	Ella Stewart	President	1
	Annette Adams	President	1
1924 Democratic	Emma Miller	President	1
	Belle Miller	President	1
	Lena Springs	Vice president	44
	Belle Miller	Vice president	3
	Maidee Renshaw	Vice president	3
	Margaret Chadbourne	Vice president	2
	Martha Bird	Vice president	1
1928 Democratic	Nellie Ross	Vice president	31
1964 Republican	Margaret C. Smith	President	27
1972 Democratic	Shirley Chisholm	President	152
	Frances Farenthold	Vice president	404
	Shirley Chisholm	Vice president	20
	Eleanor McGovern	Vice president	1
	Martha Griffiths	Vice president	1
1976 Democratic	Ellen McCormack	President	22
	Barbara Jordan	President	1
	Barbara Jordan	Vice president	28
1980 Democratic	Koryne Horbal	President	5
	Alice Tripp	President	2
1980 Republican	Anne Armstrong	President	1
1984 Democratic	Martha Kirkland	President	1
	Shirley Chisholm	Vice president	39
	Geraldine A. Ferraro	Vice president	[b]
1984 Republican	Jeane J. Kirkpatrick	Vice president	1
1992 Democratic	Patricia Schroeder	President	8

Sources: Richard C. Bain and Judith H. Parris, *Convention Decisions and Voting Records* (Washington, D.C.: The Brookings Institution, 1973); *National Party Conventions, 1831–1992* (Washington, D.C.: Congressional Quarterly Inc., 1995); and official proceedings of the Democratic and Republican conventions, 1920–1992.

[a] Fractional vote rounded to nearest whole number.
[b] Nominated by acclamation.

Figure 3-1 Political Views of Convention Delegates, Party Members, and the General Public, 1992

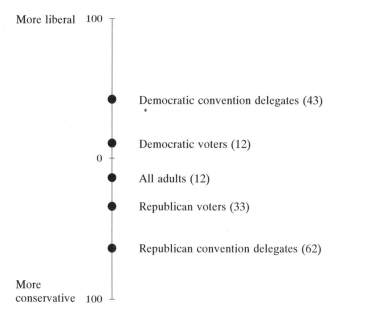

More liberal 100

Democratic convention delegates (43)

Democratic voters (12)

0

All adults (12)

Republican voters (33)

Republican convention delegates (62)

More
conservative 100

Source: New York Times/CBS News poll.

Note: Figures are derived from the difference between the percentage of those who described themselves as liberal and the percentage of those who described themselves as conservative. Scores on the top of the scale indicate a surplus of liberals; those on the bottom indicate a surplus of conservatives.

Exercises

1. Since 1956 both major parties have needed only one ballot at their national conventions to nominate a presidential candidate. However, at sixteen earlier conventions the Democrats went beyond one ballot, and the Republicans have held ten multiballot conventions.

Relying on data contained in this chapter and your own research, develop a list of common characteristics of those multiballot conventions. For example, was the party out of power? Do the 1996 Republican or Democratic conventions have any of the characteristics you have identified?

2. Credentials, rules, or platform fights often are directly related to the struggle for the nomination at major party conventions. Indeed, the votes frequently serve as accurate predictors of the presidential balloting.

Using information in this chapter, select a recent convention and compare the vote on a particular credentials, rules, or platform fight to the first-ballot vote for presidential nominees. How do the two votes relate?

3. Review the 1996 Democratic and Republican conventions. With an eye toward a successful general election campaign, list positive and negative developments at each convention.

4. Review the media coverage of the 1996 Democratic and Republican conventions. Identify themes presented by the coverage. Did these themes present positive or negative images of the proceedings? In general, what did this coverage emphasize and what did it ignore? Did media emphasis help, hurt, or not affect public perceptions of the nominees and their parties?

5. What was the impact of the 1996 major party conventions upon potential or declared

independent or third-party candidates? Did the conventions help or hurt these candidates? How?

6. You are a top aide to either the Democratic or Republican candidate who is the front-runner at the beginning of the 1996 convention. Present a memo outlining a strategy to secure the nomination and unite the party. The memo should deal with such items as credentials, rules, or platform concessions that might be appropriate, the selection of a vice presidential nominee, the substance and style of the nominee's acceptance speech, and a general strategy to deal with the media.

7. Organize a debate on the pros and cons of major party national nominating conventions. Do they continue to serve critical functions or are they outdated and unnecessary?

8. Compare a nineteenth-century national nominating convention to one in the last decade. How many of the differences can be explained by the development of a sophisticated electronic media?

9. Discuss the role of African American and women candidates at major party nominating conventions (see Tables 3-5 and 3-6). Was 1996 different?

10. In 1992 the delegates to both major party conventions were not representative of party members as a whole (see Figure 3-1). For example, Democratic delegates were substantially more liberal than party members as a whole while Republican delegates were much more conservative than party members as a whole.

Does this discrepancy matter? Is it worthwhile to pursue conventions which are not only ideologically representative but also identical to overall party membership in terms of gender, age, and class? Why? Is such a convention possible?

11. Identify a potential or declared independent or third-party candidate and review how that candidate gains access to the general election ballot in your state. Evaluate this process in your state. Is it too onerous or just about right?

Additional Sources
Printed Material and Videos

David, Paul, Ralph Goldman, and Richard C. Bain. *The Politics of National Party Conventions*. Washington, D.C.: The Brookings Institution, 1960. Perhaps the most comprehensive study to date of convention organization and decision making through the 1950s.

"Highlights of the 1992 Republican and Democratic Conventions." A video of selected speeches at the most recent Democratic and Republican conventions, including those that set the tone for each convention. Available from the Purdue University Public Affairs Video Archives.

National Party Conventions, 1831–1992. Washington, D.C.: Congressional Quarterly Inc., 1995. A handy guide to every major party convention that includes a brief review of all proceedings and key votes.

Royer, Charles T., ed. *Campaign for President: The Managers Look at '92*. Hollis, New Hampshire: Hollis Publishing Company, 1994. After each presidential election, Harvard University's Institute of Politics invites key aides of the presidential candidates and representatives of the press to discuss the recently completed campaign. The transcript of this latest discussion contains both a lively and informative inside review of what went right and wrong at the 1992 major party nominating conventions.

On-Line Data

"Democratic National Committee." This site, maintained by the Democratic Party, provides a wide array of information and data on Democratic politics. Included are audio and video excerpts from the 1992 Democratic convention and news of convention activities and events planned for the 1996 convention.

Access method: World Wide Web
To access: http://www.democrats.org/
Choose: Audio and video excerpts of the 1992 convention are available on the option identified as "What's Cool"

"1996 GOP Convention Home Page." The *San Diego Daily Transcript* has established this page on the Republican convention. It includes details on the convention center where the Republicans will convene and news of related events and activities.
Access method: World Wide Web
To access: http://www.sddt.com/files/convention.html
Choose: For convention news, try: Transcript Convention Coverage

As this pastiche of campaign buttons shows, presidential campaigns, even prior to the media age, largely were waged between simple images and slogans.

4

The Campaign Trail

General election campaigns for president have historically been rooted in two fundamental and strategic facts: these elections actually are won in an obscure body called the electoral college, and most Americans were motivated on election day by their attachment to one of the major political parties. The ongoing transformation of the presidential selection process is, however, rapidly changing the relevance and importance of both of these factors, and is redirecting campaign strategies in the process.

The Electoral College

American presidential elections are not national elections in which the candidate receiving the most popular votes wins. National popular votes are neither the basis upon which the votes in American presidential elections are counted nor the basis upon which the campaigns are conducted.

Presidents are normally elected by obtaining a majority (270) of 538 electoral votes. Almost all states allocate their total electoral votes to the candidate who receives more popular votes on a statewide basis than any other candidate. (The two exceptions, Maine and Nebraska, allot their electoral votes on both a congressional district and statewide basis.) Each state's electoral votes equal its combined number of senators and representatives. Thus, pop-

ular victories in large states, even by the narrowest of margins, become critical to a successful campaign. For example, winning California by one popular vote, and thereby receiving its fifty-four electoral votes, makes up for losing by tens of thousands of popular votes in the states of Hawaii, Alaska, Washington, Oregon, Nevada, Arizona, Utah, Idaho, Montana, and Wyoming.

As a result, the arithmetic of the electoral college has focused presidential elections on a small number of populous states. Not surprisingly, since 1968 all successful presidential candidates have won popular vote victories in, and thereby received all of the electoral votes of, at least half of the following states: California, Florida, Illinois, Michigan, New Jersey, New York, Ohio, Pennsylvania, and Texas (see Table 4-1).

For Republicans, the electoral college was good news for two decades. In the six presidential elections from 1968 to 1988, Republican presidential candidates regularly won the electoral votes of six of the critical nine states. They additionally won all of the electoral votes in these six elections in eighteen smaller states, primarily in the West and Midwest. As a result, some election analysts had come to the conclusion that Republicans had a "lock" on the electoral college that the Democrats had little hope of picking. The 1992 election both changed this prognosis and raised the possibility that the electoral college would insert new biases into the presidential selection system (see Table 4-2).

The electoral college traditionally discouraged third-party or independent candidates and legitimized popular vote victories, no matter how slight, of major party candidates. With the ongoing decline of major party loyalties and the concomitant rise of viable third-party or independent candidates, however, there is an increasing likelihood that the electoral college will operate differently. The early candidacy of independent Ross Perot (who initially withdrew in July 1992), for example, raised the possibility that each of three candidates would receive approximately one-third of the popular vote. Such a situation would not produce a majority for one candidate in the electoral college, throwing the election of the president to the House of Representatives, or would produce a winner who had received the smallest proportion of popular votes since the contested election of 1824.

The electoral college nonetheless continues to direct candidate strategies in the general election. In a three- or four-candidate race, however, these strategies are quite distinct from those in a two-candidate race. In a stable two-party system, the ultimate goal of the nominees was to amass a majority of electoral votes through the most efficient use of campaign resources. This almost always produced campaigns focusing on attaining popular vote majorities in critical large states. In a three- or four-way race in which an electoral college majority may be unattainable, candidates will be forced to gear campaigns toward the eventuality of the House of Representatives selecting the president. In this regard, campaigns will be run with the ultimate goal of influencing the vote of members of Congress. Given that there are no established criteria governing how members should vote in proceedings convened under the Twelfth Amendment, presidential candidates and campaigns will enter a very murky and virtually uncharted area of electoral politics. In multicandidate presidential races, cam-

paigns would also focus on smaller and more selective segments of the voting population, since only a bare plurality of the vote would be necessary to secure all of a state's electoral votes. In such races, nominees will not necessarily be forced to build broad coalitions of support or wage a national campaign.

Partisanship

The second important, but oft-ignored, fact about U.S. presidential elections is that voter behavior in a stable two-party system is explained significantly by partisan affinities. Voter attachment to one of the two major parties provides an enduring context in which elections are fought and general election campaigns pursued (see Table 4-3). "If," as Thomas Patterson has eloquently stated, "the campaign is to be a time for the voters to exercise their discretion, they need help in discovering what their choices represent." This help is provided primarily by political parties.

While partisanship continues to be both one of the major motivators for political participation and one of the best indicators of voter choice, it has clearly become less of an overall guide for voters. This decline in partisanship is also reflected in the fact that in every presidential election since 1968, over one-quarter of the voters have supported the presidential candidate of one party and the candidate of another for the House of Representatives. A post-World War II record 36 percent of all voters split their ballots in this fashion in 1992 (see Table 4-4).

Clearly, other factors have always modified the role partisanship plays in presidential elections. Also influencing a voter's decision are the perceived personality traits and attributes of the candidates, as well as the policy preferences of the voter. A voter's perception of a presidential candidate's basic skills and qualities is an increasingly important consideration that may modify, if not neutralize, the impact of weak partisanship. Is the candidate knowledgeable about particular issues? Could the candidate solve particular problems?

If elected, would the candidate provide strong leadership? In general, is the candidate trustworthy? A large number of voters based their vote in 1992 on these perceived attributes, strongly affecting the overall distribution of the vote. For example, President Bush won among voters who said it mattered most that a candidate "is honest or trustworthy" or "has strong convictions" (see Table 4-5).

The second factor modifying voter partisanship involves policy positions. When voters can identify their own positions with those of the candidates, strong policy voting takes place. In the 1992 election, for example, data collected by the National Election Studies of the University of Michigan and analyzed by Robert S. Erikson and Kent L. Tedin reveal a strong relationship between voters' positions on economic and foreign policy issues and their vote. Of voters who took the most liberal stances on ten economic and foreign policy issues, 92 percent voted for Clinton, while 85 percent of those who took the most conservative stances voted for Bush. Even though only a minority of voters view elections in these terms, many others may cast ballots in a more general sense on the basis of issues. Voters may not refer to this match or mismatch of policy preferences, but they may speak of the party or candidate that best represents people like them.

Broad categories of voter self-identification, such as social class, religion, gender, or race, may also affect voting decisions. The greater the intensity and importance of these affiliations, the greater their impact in establishing a stable voter identity. For example, African Americans as a group possess a predictable and identifiable partisanship and perspective on many policy issues. The Democrats' nomination of Geraldine Ferraro for vice president in 1984 prompted considerable discussion of the role gender might play in elections. In particular, people questioned whether her nomination would attract women as a group to the Democratic ticket and ultimately to the Democratic Party. It did not.

Candidate Strategies

To win the general election, candidates must develop strategies based upon party affiliation, voter perspectives on the skills and qualities of all the candidates, and voter perceptions of policy preferences of the candidates. For 1996 those strategies will also clearly depend upon the number and variety of credible candidates in the race.

In a race with a Republican opponent only, President Clinton will attempt to mobilize both traditional Democrats, who are generally liberal in orientation, and independents, who are more moderate and voted significantly for Perot in 1992. This diverse and fragile ideological coalition would be held together both by Clinton's congenial, people-oriented style and his portrayal of the Republicans as dangerously to the right of the political mainstream. The president's stances on social policy issues and the budget, in the wake of devastating Democratic losses in the 1994 midterm elections, have been clearly aimed at securing the ideological middle, with the assumption that in a two-way race with a conservative Republican, liberals have only one choice. Republicans would counter that they are the party of change, as reflected in the passage of an ambitious agenda after they regained control of Congress in 1994. A Republican victory would merely be a further pursuit of this agenda. No doubt, Republicans would additionally raise the specter of numerous ethical scandals haunting the Democratic administration.

A race including a third-party candidate or independent of the left or the middle would complicate election strategies, especially for the president. With an independent candidacy of the middle, launched by Perot or by retired general Colin Powell, President Clinton could theoretically be reelected with the votes of traditional Democratic constituencies such as labor union members, Jews, African Americans, and lower socioeconomic groups. This would, however, require some effort by the president to move quickly to the left, reaffirming the role of an activist government, in order to soothe frustrated liberals in the Democratic Party. An independent or third-party challenge from the left would require the president to expend more resources to secure moderate and conservative Democrats and independents, who are predominantly white and middle-class. The implications for the Republican nominee of third-party or independent candidates are equally critical. An independent candidate of the middle, for example, would relieve the Republican nominee of the burden of having to attract moderate support after a primary campaign clearly dominated by conservatives.

Whether specific campaign strategies are successful hinges on the ability of the respective campaigns to control the terms of debate and thereby alter voter perspectives in their favor. In this regard, the general election campaign may be viewed as a series of both planned and unplanned events that influence voter perspectives and ultimately guide voter behavior on election day.

Dire economic or international events that occur before the formal start of the general election campaign may persuade voters that a change is necessary. President Carter, for example, entered the 1980 election campaign with a lingering crisis in Iran. Press reports on the American hostages provided daily public reminders of Carter's foreign policy failures. Similarly, President Clinton's ability to convince voters of his leadership skills in both foreign and domestic policy will depend upon developments in the Middle East, the former Soviet Union, and the Balkans and on the state of the American economy (see Figures 4-1 and 4-2).

The Mass Media's Role

The primacy of partisanship in presidential elections logically corresponded with the dominance of political parties in American politics. Parties reinforced partisan behavior by controlling the content and distribution of political information to citizens. Party decline is a complex and multifaceted phenomenon. One critical part of this change has been the development of independent media that dominate the provision both of specific information about candidates and campaigns and of a general perspective on the entire political process. It is this new role for the media that best explains contemporary trends in voter behavior and candidate strategies.

Voters now receive most of their information about candidates and the campaign through mass media that is particularly oriented toward human interest stories of conflict and travail, centered around an individual episode. The media have additionally become more journalist-centered: greater time and space are spent on the journalist's interpretation of events than on the words or deeds of the newsmaker. This approach to the news has particular consequences for media coverage of elections.

The preferred election story covers who is up or down in the race, conflict within or between campaigns, or the personal travails of a candidate. Little information is conveyed about policy issues, and the general orientation of most stories is increasingly negative. Stories are primarily conveyed to the audience by a notable journalist, with less than ten seconds provided for quotes or "bites" from the candidate or his or her spokesperson. Good visuals are also a requirement of each story. The changing orientation toward negativity is reflected in the titles of stories in the major weekly news magazines. In the 1960 campaign, for example, *Time* and *Newsweek* did not include a single negative title on the major candidates. In the 1992 campaign, titles in these same magazines included "Is Bill Clinton for Real?" and "Nobody's Perfect: The Doubts about Ross Perot."

This type of coverage is correlated with declining voter knowledge of policy issues and with increased negative perspectives toward all candidates and government. Additionally, the media have been unable to generate the levels of voter interest and participation once routinely facilitated by strong political parties and partisanship.

Candidates and campaigns have been forced to operate within the new and developing rules of media coverage; they must make "news" according to the media's own criteria. Such news may include a variety of planned events, such as a speech to a receptive audience, the release of polling results, or the announcement of the receipts of a fund-raiser. For incumbent presidents running for reelection, news making is one of the perks of office. For example, President Clinton's central role in pursuing a peace in the Middle East and fostering a tolerable resolution of the conflicts in the former Soviet Union and the Balkans provides numerous publicity advantages over campaign rivals.

The president also can gain positive publicity over rivals through his role in setting the nation's legislative agenda. For example, President Bush's April 1991 announcement of proposed reforms of the public school system not only confronted a national problem but also served to protect Bush from campaign charges of weak leadership on the domestic front. President Clinton's unveiling in June 1995 of his own plan for a balanced budget gave him the opportunity to reposition himself against his Republican opposition.

Even when candidates and campaigns are mindful of the contemporary requirements of positive coverage by the media, the best-laid plans can go awry. Unplanned events can make or break a campaign. Most common are unplanned events that raise new issues or reinforce old ones. For example, Republican nominee Dan Quayle's lackluster performance during the 1988 vice presidential debate reinforced widespread public perceptions that he was not qualified for office. In 1992, the ongoing series of alleged improprieties related to Governor Clinton's private life periodically reaffirmed the "character issue" while Ross Perot's patronizing remarks to the national convention of the National Association for the Advancement of Colored People raised accusations of insensitivity.

The 1992 campaign reaffirmed the critical role of the media in deciding winners and generally defining the terms of campaign discourse, but it also saw some important changes in the relationship between candidates and the media. These changes took place because of increasing concerns by candidates that they had lost control to media and because new media formats and outlets were available, and they were most prominently reflected in candidates' emphasis on less traditional news formats. These new formats often provided direct interaction between candidate and audience, which lessened the potential role of the journalist or host in structuring the "news" in a way that might be unfavorable or unflattering to the candidate. Some labeled the election the "Talk Show Campaign." President Bush, who was at first skeptical of this style of campaigning, appeared during one week with Larry King, Bryant Gumbel, Katie Couric, Charlie Gibson, Harry Smith and Paula Zahn, Sam Donaldson, and David Frost. This trend was also reflected in the increasing use by candidates of new media technology that allowed them to circumvent, if not altogether ignore, journalists: satellite communications that could beam a message directly to voters or local cable stations, "800" telephone numbers to disperse campaign information or actual recordings of the candidate's major speeches, and computer bulletin boards that fielded questions from voters to the candidate.

Paid campaign advertising was also affected by increased candidate efforts to control and hold the audience. Virtually all candidates distributed campaign videos that voters could watch at any time at their own pace. Independent candidate Perot even purchased, at a cost of $1 million, two thirty-minute prime-time slots to air "infomercials" of him presenting his views on critical issues such as the economy.

In sum, the mass media continue to set the general context of an election. The style and variety of media programming both reinforce prevailing biases in the content and orientation of election news and create new opportunities for candidates to escape this bias. Indeed, successful candidates, like successful politicians in general, are often those who are most adept at innovation within the rapidly changing world of telecommunications.

A campaign for the presidency therefore occurs within a variety of ever-changing constraints, many of which are not directly amenable to manipulation by the candidates. The matter of money is also an issue. The Federal Election Commission has estimated for 1996 that party nominees in the general election will be limited to expenditures of approximately $60 million. Although the national parties, state parties, and independent groups may spend above the limit on behalf of the candidates, campaigns and their increasing mass media emphasis are expensive. In particular, the high cost of prime-time media advertising forces candidates to make crucial choices as to which voters and media markets to target. The Clinton campaign developed a formula to help make

these difficult decisions and in the process coined a new phrase for 1992— "Cost per persuadable voter."

Beyond working adeptly within and around the ever-changing strategic constraints, the successful campaign may hinge on little more than luck. One wonders, for example, what the 1980 election results would have been if President Carter had been able to retrieve the American hostages from Iran shortly before the election, or what the dynamics of the 1992 general election would have been if the enigmatic Ross Perot had not dropped out and essentially endorsed Governor Clinton in the midst of an already successful Democratic convention. Similarly, the present international situation contains numerous unpredictable actors who could either enhance or diminish Bill Clinton's chances for reelection.

Table 4-1   State-by-State Electoral College Vote, 1968–1992

State	1996 Electoral votes	Winning party						
		1968	1972	1976	1980	1984	1988	1992
Alabama	9	AI	R	D	R	R	R	R
Alaska	3	R	R	R	R	R	R	R
Arizona	8	R	R	R	R	R	R	R
Arkansas	6	AI	R	D	R	R	R	D
California	54	R	R	R	R	R	R	D
Colorado	8	R	R	R	R	R	R	D
Connecticut	8	D	R	R	R	R	R	D
Delaware	3	R	R	D	R	R	R	D
District of Columbia	3	D	D	D	D	D	D	D
Florida	25	R	R	D	R	R	R	R
Georgia	13	AI	R	D	D	R	R	D
Hawaii	4	D	R	D	D	R	D	D
Idaho	4	R	R	R	R	R	R	R
Illinois	22	R	R	R	R	R	R	D
Indiana	12	R	R	R	R	R	R	R
Iowa	7	R	R	R	R	R	D	D
Kansas	6	R	R	R	R	R	R	R
Kentucky	8	R	R	D	R	R	R	D
Louisiana	9	AI	R	D	R	R	R	D
Maine	4	D	R	R	R	R	R	D
Maryland	10	D	R	D	D	R	R	D
Massachusetts	12	D	D	D	R	R	D	D
Michigan	18	D	R	R	R	R	R	D
Minnesota	10	D	R	D	D	D	D	D
Mississippi	7	AI	R	D	R	R	R	R

Xerox table 4.1
pp. 54-55. Note it as on
2 PAGES + then Make 15 Copies
of it with The table -- Republican
Electoral Lock on The separate
sheet -- one the other side....

Table 4-1 *Continued*

State	1996 Electoral votes	Winning party						
		1968	1972	1976	1980	1984	1988	1992
Missouri	11	R	R	D	R	R	R	D
Montana	3	R	R	R	R	R	R	D
Nebraska	5	R	R	R	R	R	R	R
Nevada	4	R	R	R	R	R	R	D
New Hampshire	4	R	R	R	R	R	R	D
New Jersey	15	R	R	R	R	R	R	D
New Mexico	5	R	R	R	R	R	R	D
New York	33	D	R	D	R	R	D	D
North Carolina	14	R[a]	R	D	R	R	R	R
North Dakota	3	R	R	R	R	R	R	R
Ohio	21	R	R	D	R	R	R	D
Oklahoma	8	R	R	R	R	R	R	R
Oregon	7	R	R	R	R	R	D	D
Pennsylvania	23	D	R	D	R	R	R	D
Rhode Island	4	D	R	D	D	R	D	D
South Carolina	8	R	R	D	R	R	R	R
South Dakota	3	R	R	R	R	R	R	R
Tennessee	11	R	R	D	R	R	R	D
Texas	32	D	R	D	R	R	R	R
Utah	5	R	R	R	R	R	R	R
Vermont	3	R	R	R	R	R	R	D
Virginia	13	R	R[a]	R	R	R	R	R
Washington	11	D	R	R[a]	R	R	D	D
West Virginia	5	D	R	D	D	R	D	D
Wisconsin	11	R	R	D	R	R	D[a]	D
Wyoming	3	R	R	R	R	R	R	R

Source: Presidential Elections, 1789–1992 (Washington, D.C.: Congressional Quarterly Inc., 1995), 78.

Note: AI = American Independent; R = Republican; D = Democratic.

[a] Includes faithless elector who did not support candidate winning popular majority in state.

Table 4-2 Popular Vote versus Electoral College Vote, 1968–1992

Election	Candidates	Party	Popular vote	Electoral vote
1968	Richard Nixon	R	31,785,480	301
	Hubert H. Humphrey	D	31,275,166	191
	George C. Wallace	AI	9,906,473	46
1972	Richard Nixon	R	47,169,911	520
	George McGovern	D	29,170,383	17
1976	Jimmy Carter	D	40,830,763	297
	Gerald R. Ford	R	39,147,793	240
1980	Ronald Reagan	R	43,904,153	489
	Jimmy Carter	D	35,483,883	49
	John B. Anderson	I	5,720,060	0

Continued on next page

Table 4-2   *Continued*

Election	Candidates	Party	Popular vote	Electoral vote
1984	Ronald Reagan	R	54,455,075	525
	Walter F. Mondale	D	37,577,185	13
1988	George Bush	R	48,886,097	426
	Michael S. Dukakis	D	41,809,074	111
1992	George Bush	R	39,103,882	168
	Bill Clinton	D	44,909,326	370
	Ross Perot	I	19,741,657	0

Source: Presidential Elections, 1789–1992 (Washington, D.C.: Congressional Quarterly Inc., 1995), 68–74, 122–128.

Note: R = Republican; D = Democratic; AI = American Independent; I = Independent.

Table 4-3   Vote for Presidential Candidates by Party Identification, 1968–1992

Election	Candidates	Democrats	Republicans	Independents
1968	Hubert H. Humphrey (D)	74 %	9 %	31 %
	Richard Nixon (R)	12	86	44
	George C. Wallace (AI)	14	5	25
1972	George McGovern (D)	67	5	31
	Richard Nixon (R)	33	95	69
1976	Jimmy Carter (D)	82	9	38
	Gerald R. Ford (R)	18	91	57
	Eugene J. McCarthy (I)	—	—	4
1980	Jimmy Carter (D)	69	8	29
	Ronald Reagan (R)	26	86	55
	John B. Anderson (I)	4	5	14
1984	Walter F. Mondale (D)	79	4	33
	Ronald Reagan (R)	21	96	67
1988	Michael S. Dukakis (D)	85	7	43
	George Bush (R)	15	93	57
1992	Bill Clinton (D)	82	7	39
	George Bush (R)	8	77	30
	Ross Perot (I)	10	16	31

Source: Gallup Organization.

Note: D = Democratic; R = Republican; AI = American Independent; I = Independent; — = less than 1 percent. Percentages have been rounded to the nearest whole number.

Table 4-4 Public Support for the Major Parties, 1952–1992

Year	Identify with a party	Is neutral toward both parties	Is positive toward one party and negative toward the other	Split ticket between president and representative
1952	75%	13%	50%	12%
1956	73	16	40	16
1960	75	17	41	14
1964	77	20	38	15
1968	70	17	38	26
1972	64	30	30	30
1976	63	31	31	25
1980	64	37	27	34
1984	64	36	31	25
1988	63	30	34	25
1992	61	32	34	36

Source: SRC/CPS National Election Studies; Martin P. Wattenberg, *The Decline of American Political Parties, 1952–1992* (Cambridge, Mass.: Harvard University Press, 1994).

Table 4-5 Considerations in Casting a Vote, 1992

Option	Voters who said option mattered	Clinton's share of vote among voters choosing option	Bush's share of vote among voters choosing option	Perot's share of vote among voters choosing option
Will bring about needed change	38%	59%	19%	22%
Has the best plan for the country	25	52	26	21
Has the right experience	18	23	63	14
Would have good judgment in a crisis	15	26	63	11
Cares about people like me	14	57	24	20
Is honest and trustworthy	14	30	49	21
Has strong convictions	14	34	42	24
His choice of vice president	8	63	25	12
Is my party's candidate	5	47	40	12

Source: Voter Research & Survey.

Note: The question was, "Which candidate qualities mattered most in deciding how you voted?" Respondents could choose more than one option.

Table 4-6 Characteristics of Voters in States with Greatest Electoral Votes, 1992

Characteristic	California	New York	Texas
Gender			
Female	53%	52%	52%
Male	47	48	48
Age			
18–29	20	19	26
30–44	39	37	40
45–59	24	22	20
60+	18	22	14
Race			
White	79	84	74
Black	6	10	13
Hispanic	8	5	10
Asian	4	1	1
Other	2	—	1
Religion			
Protestant	29	24	45
Catholic	29	44	23
Other Christian	16	6	19
Jewish	5	17	2
Other/none	22	9	12
Income			
Less than $15,000	13	11	13
$15,000-$29,999	18	23	27
$30,000-$49,999	29	28	31
$56,000-$74,999	23	23	21
More than $75,000	16	15	9
Education			
Did not complete high school	7	5	5
High school graduate	18	24	22
Some college	31	25	31
College graduate	27	29	27
Postgraduate	16	17	15
Party affiliation			
Democrat	41	42	37
Republican	36	32	36
Independent/other	22	26	26
Ideology			
Conservative	26	25	40
Moderate	50	52	43
Liberal	23	23	17

Source: Voter Research & Survey.

Notes: Some columns total less than 100 percent because respondents did not know or refused to answer; — = less than 1 percent.

Figure 4-1 Consumer Confidence Preceding the 1980, 1984, 1992, and 1996 Elections

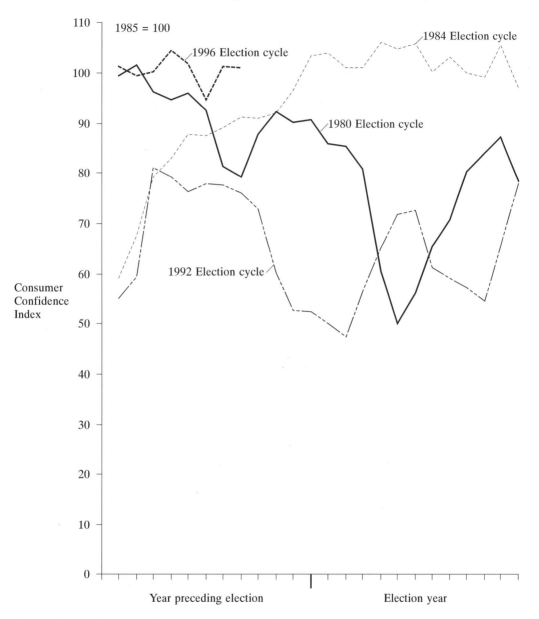

Source: The Conference Board/NFO Research.

Note: The Conference Board's Consumer Confidence Index is a monthly measurement of consumer confidence, including both evaluations of the present economic situation and expectations for the future. Since its inception in 1967, the index hit a high of 142.3 in October 1968 and a low of 43.2 in December 1974. In general, an index below 80 signals that consumers are nervous; below 70 indicates a recession. A number above 100 signals that consumers are optimistic.

Figure 4-2   Presidential Approval Ratings Preceding the 1980, 1984, 1992, and 1996 Elections

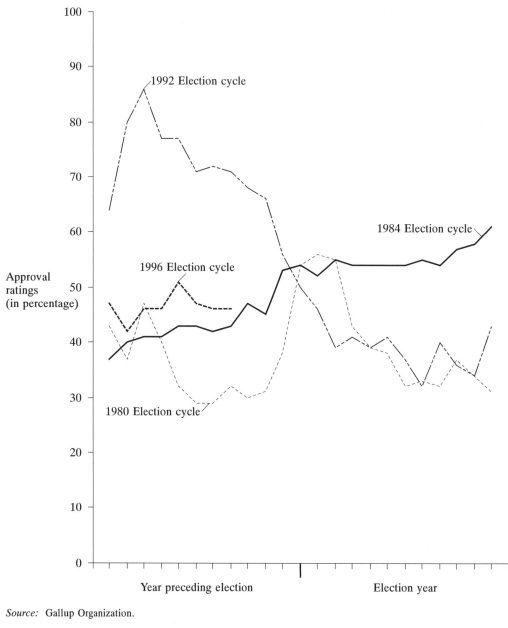

Source: Gallup Organization.

Note: Question: Do you approve or disapprove of the way _____ is handling his job as president?

Exercises

1. Review the 1996 general election campaign, focusing on unplanned events that affected the outcome of the election. What were these events? How did each candidate deal with them? Which candidate did they help and which candidate did they hurt?

2. Poll your classmates on their general election choice. Ask what they perceive the skills and characteristics of each candidate to be, how their policy positions compare with those of each candidate, and what their party affiliations are.

Review the results, identifying the strongest correlates of support for each candidate. Which factor appears to be most important—perception of candidate skills and characteristics, perception of the match of candidate and respondent positions on issues, or party affiliation?

3. Review several general campaign advertisements. Identify both the stated and unstated assertions of the ad. Are these assertions correct?

4. Write a script for a thirty-second television advertisement for any of the major candidates in the 1996 general election. Identify the particular media markets where the ad would be most appropriate. Explain why.

5. Using information found in Table 4-6, develop a campaign strategy for any major candidate in California, New York, and Texas—the three states with the largest number of electoral votes. The campaign should be tailored to the particular characteristics of voters in those states. Which groups of voters should the campaign emphasize? What issues could be used to mobilize these voters?

6. After completing exercise 5, develop a national campaign strategy for any major party or independent candidate in the 1996 general election.

First, identify a strategy to achieve a majority of 270 electoral votes. This strategy should include the states and groups of voters that the campaign will emphasize and the issues

that will be used to mobilize these voters. Second, develop another strategy that assumes the electoral college will be deadlocked and the selection of the president will be made by the House of Representatives. What states will be targeted and why? What kinds of direct or indirect appeals will be made to members of the House of Representatives who will ultimately select the president?

7. Review a selection of campaign advertisements by the major candidates to identify the themes of the 1996 campaign. Can the election results be explained by the success, or lack of success, of these themes?

8. Using Figures 4-1 and 4-2, compare presidential popularity and consumer confidence during the 1996 election with those during the 1980, 1984, and 1992 elections, in which incumbents also were running for reelection. Can the results of the 1996 election be explained by the levels of popular support for President Clinton and consumer confidence in the economy preceding the election?

9. Choose a state and analyze the results of the presidential election. How did particular regions of the state or groups within the state vote? Identify issues and candidate positions that may have determined the results.

10. Political scientists have identified "critical elections" as ones in which the landscape of American politics is transformed. A different political party becomes the dominant party when voters in large number change their political affiliations or when new voters enter the political arena. Drastic changes in the composition of the House of Representatives and the Senate often accompany such a shift. Can the 1996 election be considered a critical election? Why or why not?

11. Review the role of third-party or independent candidates in the 1996 election. What role did they play in the campaign and election?

12. Identify new telecommunications technology that was used by candidates during the 1996 general election. What was the impact of this technology upon the outcome of the elec-

tion? What was the relationship between candidates and the media?

13. Review and evaluate the role that the media performed in the 1996 general election. What was different compared to past elections? Do you consider these differences to be positive or negative changes? Explain.

Additional Sources

Printed Material and Videos

Berns, Walter, ed. *After the People Vote: A Guide to the Electoral College*. Washington, D.C.: AEI Press, 1992. A concise review of the relevant constitutional provisions and state statutes governing the workings of the electoral college. This small book also contains two interpretative essays by Martin Diamond and Norman Ornstein.

"The Best General Commercials of 1992." Videos of sixty-three of the most notable campaign commercials from the 1992 general election, available from Aristotle in Washington, D.C. An invaluable supplement to studying an increasingly critical aspect of campaigning.

Erikson, Robert S., and Kent L. Tedin. *American Public Opinion*. Needham Heights, Mass.: Allyn and Bacon, 1995. This book contains an excellent chapter on public opinion and presidential voting with data from the 1992 election.

Iyengar, Shanto. *Is Anyone Responsible?: How Television Frames Political Issues*. Chicago: University of Chicago Press, 1991. A ground-breaking analysis of the impact of television on public attitudes.

Patterson, Thomas E. *Out of Order*. New York: Knopf, 1993. What happens when the media attempt to perform critical political functions related to selecting the president? Patterson reviews what he considers to be this inappropriate role for the media.

Wattenberg, Martin P. *The Decline of American Political Parties, 1952–1992*. Cambridge, Mass.: Harvard University Press, 1994. A systematic and thorough argument that the public increasingly views parties as irrelevant.

On-Line Data

"The C-Span Networks Home Page." This site provides ongoing coverage of the presidential campaign as well as a review of all C-Span programming. It is ideal for following the details of the campaign in its final stages.

Access method: World Wide Web
To access: http://www.c-span.org/
Choose: Campaign '96

"Pathfinder." This site, updated daily, contains on-line news articles written for Time Warner publications. A significant number of these articles relate to politics; many focus on the 1996 election.

Access Method: World Wide Web
To Access: http://www.timeinc.com
Choose: Scroll to News Features and then to Campaign '96. This site also allows users to search the Time Warner database for articles of interest.

Vice President Dan Quayle presides over a joint session of Congress January 6, 1993, certifying the election of Bill Clinton as president and Al Gore as vice president. Sen. Wendell H. Ford (left) and House Speaker Thomas S. Foley (right) assist in examining the electoral vote tally.

5

Controversies for the Future

Characteristic of American politics is periodic review of its most fundamental institutions. This reevaluation, often called "reform," may portray particular institutions as hopelessly flawed, undemocratic, unrepresentative, unaccountable, or inefficient.

Areas of Controversy

The laws, customs, and practices that govern the way Americans elect their chief executive are not exempt from reevaluation. Numerous controversial aspects of the presidential selection process have come under increasing scrutiny. Some parts of the process have changed much and still are under attack. Others have changed little despite continued and vociferous criticism.

Both the 1992 presidential election and the 1994 midterm elections reflected widespread dissatisfaction with "politics as usual." This dissatisfaction has prompted proposals for change in virtually every aspect of the electoral process. Although general dissatisfaction runs increasingly deep among the electorate, the disparate and often contradictory sources of this discontent have failed to produce a consensus on what exact changes should be made in electoral laws and procedures. Nonetheless, declining support for the major parties, increasing anti-Washington and anti-central government sentiments, and continuing concern about issue-

less campaigns depressing citizen participation have all helped to focus public attention on the need for electoral reform.

Proposals for change have focused specifically on citizen access to registration and the vote, candidate access to the ballot, the role of government in campaign finance, the influence of the media on campaigns, and the mechanisms that translate citizen preferences into successful candidacies.

Access to the Ballot: Voters

The qualifications for registration and voting have varied throughout American history. African Americans, for example, enjoyed suffrage in the period directly after the Civil War. By the turn of the century, however, most had been effectively excluded from the polling booth. This situation changed once again with the civil rights movement in the 1960s.

In the last several decades, the trend has been toward a registration and voting process that is increasingly open. The Nineteenth Amendment to the Constitution gave women the vote in 1920 and African Americans were effectively enfranchised in 1965 by the Voting Rights Act. In 1972 the Twenty-sixth Amendment extended the vote to eighteen-to-twenty-year-olds. Hispanics and other language minorities were enfranchised in 1975 by amendments to the Voting Rights Act. Additionally, the Equal Access to Voting Rights Act of 1984 made the registration and voting process more accessible to the infirm and the handicapped.

Despite the removal of a number of barriers to participation, many eligible citizens still do not register or vote (see Table 5-1). Even though turnout of the eligible voting population increased in 1992, the level of participation compared unfavorably to almost every European democracy and remained low even for U.S. presidential elections.

This continuing low level of participation prompted Congress in 1993 to pass further legislation that would make registration easier and ultimately, it was hoped, increase the number of voters. The National Voter Registration Act of 1993 requires states to allow residents to register by mail or when they apply for a driver's license and to make registration forms available at agencies that provide public assistance.

Fueled by a widespread concern about low levels of registration and voting, this bill nonetheless ran counter to another theme in contemporary electoral reform—anti-Washington and anti-central government sentiment. The result was resistance by a dozen or more states to what they considered unfunded federal mandates. Indeed, the federal government had to sue several states to force them to comply with the new law.

As a result of this increasing hostility to federally mandated efforts to increase registration and voting, most other election reforms have not moved beyond the committee stage in Congress. Although hearings have been held on proposals to establish early voting, mail voting, and telephone voting, most successful legislative efforts have occurred at the state level.

By 1994 at least nine states had adopted some variant of early voting involving either unrestricted absentee voting or the casting of ballots at polling places set up prior to election day. In 1993 Oregon held statewide elections entirely by mail and is considering conducting all elections in the state that way. In 1994 Idaho, New Hampshire, and Wyoming implemented election day registration. Other states are considering additional innovations such as registration or registration and voting via fax.

Proponents of these changes believe that making registration and voting easier would bring millions more Americans to the polls. Others, however, assert that the sources of citizen nonparticipation are varied and therefore not amenable to a quick fix. For example, the Committee for the Study of the American Electorate concluded in its review of registration and voting in the 1992 presidential election that "[e]nhancing the ability for citizens to register assures them of the opportunity to vote, but it is motivation that will actually bring them to vote."

Access to the Ballot: Candidates

Dominance of American electoral politics by the two major parties has produced federal and state laws that provide easy, if not guaranteed, access to the ballot for major party candidates while imposing onerous restrictions upon independent or third-party candidates. Decline in public support for the two major parties and a growing number of successful minor party or independent candidates, however, have placed increased pressure upon these laws and regulations.

Although Congress has held hearings on legislation to make it easier for independent and third-party candidates for federal office to get on the ballot, growing opposition to imposing additional ballot requirements upon the states has slowed such efforts at the federal level. In contrast, activity on the state level has been intense. In early 1995, bills that would change the existing ballot requirements for independent or third-party candidates were introduced in more than two dozen state legislatures.

Changes in this area of state election law, however, have not been entirely in the direction of easier access to the ballot. For example, in April 1995 ballot access reform was defeated in Florida; in May most of the barriers to the ballot for third-party and independent candidates were lowered in Colorado.

Ballot access issues have also been pursued in the state and federal courts, where, again, results have been mixed. In March 1995 a U.S. District Court upheld the Georgia presidential primary ballot access law, which allows a committee of state government officials and party leaders to approve candidates for the primary ballot. There are no alternative means via petitioning or filing fees for candidates to gain access to the ballot.

Campaign Finance

Although money may be the "mother's milk" of politics, it nonetheless has been the source of increasing controversy. The $550 million in presidential election-related spending in 1992 and the increasing number of loopholes used by candidates to elude federal campaign finance laws have only furthered the debate. The adoption of new technologies has caused campaign costs to rise dramatically. Voters now are more likely to be swayed by an expensive prime-time television advertisement than by an unpaid campaign worker knocking at their door. A private jet now is the most likely mode of transportation for candidates, while the slower and less expensive whistle-stop tour is but a piece of nostalgia. In sum, critics have charged that candidates with greater financial resources have increasingly unfair advantages, and that the individuals and organizations who provide those resources exert too great an influence in the electoral process. In response to these criticisms, Congress moved in the 1970s to regulate money in presidential elections. The 1971 Federal Election Campaign Act was followed by amendments in 1974, 1976, and 1979 and by several Supreme Court decisions that altered some of its provisions.

Current federal campaign finance law provides partial public funding to presidential primary candidates and public grants to major party candidates in the general election campaign (approximately $60 million to each nominee in 1996). In return for public funds, candidates agree to spending limits in both the prenomination and general election campaigns. Additionally, individuals are permitted to contribute no more than $1,000 to any presidential

candidate running in the primary election campaign and are prohibited from contributing directly to any presidential candidate in the general election. The law also allots $3 million plus cost-of-living adjustments to each major party to finance its national convention (approximately $26 million in 1996) and allows, but limits, national party expenditures on behalf of a candidate (approximately $11.6 million in 1996). Finally, the Federal Election Commission has the authority to review the eligibility of presidential candidates for public funds, to certify payment of those funds, and to audit all public funding recipients to make sure that funds were spent in compliance with the law.

Significant limitations, however, undercut the effectiveness of the Federal Election Campaign Act and its amendments. Most prominently, several kinds of contributions to candidates and expenditures by or on behalf of candidates either are not regulated or are regulated by distinctly loose standards. For example, money raised or spent by national political parties is not regulated for a variety of activities that affect presidential campaigns on the state and local levels. Such money, popularly designated "soft money," is designed to support solely state and local party activities, but sorting out expenditures for purely local activities is difficult. In states with minimal campaign finance regulation, this has meant both unlimited contributions and expenditures on activities that are an integral part of presidential campaigns. The two national parties raised $47.7 million in 1988 and $67.8 million in 1992 in soft money contributions to support local and state party activities in conjunction with the presidential campaigns of their nominees. The national parties reported that over two hundred of these contributions in the period 1991–92 were in amounts of $100,000 or more.

In addition, political action committees (PACs), which are established specifically to raise and spend money in federal elections, are an available source of funds before and during the presidential campaign. Leadership PACs, committees organized by prospective presidential candidates, have become a critical source of organizational resources and funds in the precampaign period (see Table 5-2). By avoiding the expenditure limits of the Federal Election Campaign Act, they allow potential candidates to pursue effectively what one scholar labels "The Shadow Campaign."

Additionally, the Federal Election Campaign Act regulates formal PAC giving by standards more liberal than those for individuals. Under federal law, individuals may contribute only $1,000 to a presidential primary contender; PACs may contribute five times as much. Individuals may contribute no more than a total of $25,000 to candidates in any one calendar year; no aggregate limit has been set on PAC giving. Equally important is that no restrictions exist on independent spending by PACs (or by individuals) on behalf of or against presidential candidates.

In the last several elections, PACs have served as precampaign vehicles but have also spent independently in support of or in opposition to presidential candidates or contributed directly to presidential campaigns where permitted by law. From 1991 to 1992 these independent expenditures amounted to approximately $4 million, while direct contributions totalled $800,000. PACS may also influence presidential campaigns by directing unregulated or soft money to state and local activities.

The use of soft money and PACs in presidential campaigns reflects a broader problem in the Federal Election Campaign Act—inadequate regulated monies fueling the search for additional monies to fund presidential campaigns. Campaign costs have risen rapidly while the value of the dollar has declined. Yet the contribution limit on individual giving to campaigns has remained the same. The maximum $1,000 individual contribution has lost more than half its value since the inception of the limit in 1975. Furthermore, state and aggregate limits on campaign spending are increasingly unrealistic and public funding for presidential campaigns inadequate. In sum, the state of presidential campaign finance, according to

many, is approaching a crisis situation comparable to Watergate, which spawned the current law.

Despite these concerns, Congress has been unable to reach agreement on solutions, and public support for a role for Washington in campaign finance continues to wane. In the 103d Congress, despite the fact that President Clinton presented his own campaign finance proposals and the House and the Senate passed their own versions of campaign finance reform, no legislation ultimately emerged. The major sticking point was new restrictions on PAC giving in congressional races. Congress did move in the summer of 1993 to avert a shortfall in the tax check-off program, which provides public monies for the presidential campaign, by increasing the individual check-off from one dollar to three dollars. In the Republican-controlled 104th Congress, campaign finance reform has been a low priority and has therefore been approached in a piecemeal fashion. For example, as part of budget-cutting efforts, the Senate Budget Committee recommended that public financing of presidential campaigns be abolished. This recommendation was defeated 56-44, with two presidential candidates, Sens. Bob Dole and Phil Gramm, voting to kill the public financing system. In June 1995 President Clinton proposed that campaign finance reform be addressed by an eight-member commission on political reform.

In the meantime, public support for Washington-based solutions to campaign finance problems has declined significantly. Campaign finance legislation was originally designed to level the financial playing field with a combination of federal restrictions and monies, but public perception of such legislation now differs. Indeed, the general public perception of independent Ross Perot, whose 1992 presidential campaign was self-financed, was not of a "fat cat" buying an election but of an individual whose wealth allowed him to remain free from corrupting federal influence and monies. Declining public participation in the tax check-off program, which ultimately forced Congress to raise the check-off amount, is but another sign that the public's conception of campaign finance reform includes a shrinking role for Washington and central government.

The Media's Role

Another source of controversy is the powerful role that the mass media perform in conveying information to the public about the entire presidential selection process. From evaluating specific candidates to providing general cues about politics, the mass media have become one of the most important players in presidential campaigns.

This increasingly critical role has generally been accepted as a fact of life in American politics. Certain circumstances, however, have triggered severe criticism and have led concerned citizens and Congress to look for ways to refashion or reform the part played by the media. For example, in the 1988 and 1992 presidential elections, media-generated controversies focusing on the private side of candidates' lives led to campaigns in which discussions of public policy issues were often eclipsed.

After what was generally evaluated to be poor coverage of policy issues during the 1988 campaign, even the media promised to do better. Some changes in their campaign coverage, such as newspapers' careful and systematic scrutiny of campaign advertisements (labeled by some as "truth boxes") did occur in 1992. However, by the time of the general election, the overall number of stories on network evening newscasts that focused on policy issues was even smaller than in 1988. According to the Center for Media and Public Affairs, policy-oriented stories accounted for only 32 percent of all stories, compared to 40 percent in the same period of the campaign in 1988.

Ongoing complaints about increasing media interest in the personal foibles of candidates or in campaign strategies rather than substantive discussion of policy differences among the candidates is part of a larger critique of the overall role of the American mass media in the political process. Many have argued that the changing definition of "news" by the media has led to a precipitous decline in the quality of political debate and discussion that is most starkly exhibited in presidential campaigns. In 1992 the mainstream media were preoccupied with an alleged extramarital affair by Governor Clinton, despite the fact that the allegation was first raised by a tabloid newspaper. After watching a recording of the first Kennedy-Nixon debate in 1960, one reviewer of the American political scene recently wrote that the exchange was so superior to contemporary campaign discussion that he felt "as if this presidential debate were happening in some other culture."

Although the decline in the quality of public discourse is related to a variety of complex and interrelated changes in American society, the focus of campaign reform efforts to improve it periodically returns to the mass media. Suggestions for improvement have included increased governmental regulation of the media, increased candidate access to the media, and creation of alternative media sources of information for the public. Legislation introduced in the 103d Congress would have required debates between all presidential and vice presidential candidates receiving public financing.

Although it has been somewhat muted since 1988, criticism also remains of the media's reporting of voting trends or prediction of winners before the polls have closed. In particular, western Democrats have charged that network predictions, before the polls had closed in the West on election night in 1980, of candidate Ronald Reagan's victory over President Jimmy Carter kept many Democrats from voting, thereby damaging Democratic candidates for the Senate and the House of Representatives. This controversy has since simmered, with the networks again declaring a winner in 1984 before polls had closed in western states. The networks ultimately agreed that, beginning in 1986, they would not predict winners in particular states until the polls had closed, although this policy did not prevent them from yet again declaring a national winner in 1988 and 1992 before polls had closed in some western states. Many in Congress assert that the only real solution is to establish a uniform schedule of voting throughout the nation. With this goal in mind, legislation has been introduced that would require all polls in the continental United States to close at 9:00 p.m. eastern standard time in presidential election years.

Despite the introduction of numerous pieces of legislation in Congress to deal with these controversies, change in the role of the media in the presidential selection process is unlikely to occur through government regulation. To begin with, the controversy has cooled somewhat because the relationship between candidates and the media is changing as the media itself is undergoing a rapid transformation. Many candidates are now convinced that they can successfully navigate the new media to secure both nomination and election. Additionally, overall telecommunications reform pending in Congress will most likely diminish the role of government in regulation of the media and thereby set the standard for any future reforms related specifically to the performance of the media in the presidential selection process. Finally, the debate over reform of the media hinges to a large degree on an even more sensitive and difficult question: In a nation with a free press, what degree of government regulation of the mass media is tolerable?

Translating Votes into Victories

Finally, also at issue is the formal process through which citizen preferences are translated into winning and losing candidates. Preferences for major party candidates may be translated directly into votes for presidential nominees at national party conventions through primaries or caucuses or indirectly through the appointment of party officials or notables as delegates. Supporters of independent or third-party candidates may also hold nominating conventions and use primaries to select participants in these conventions, although in most cases they secure actual nomination through a state-by-state ballot petition process.

Defenders of the current nomination process argue that it provides an effective means of winnowing the field of candidates while maintaining broad-based national parties, which are necessary to govern the nation. Critics assert that the entire process should be fundamentally altered or abolished because most citizens do not participate, those who do are not necessarily representative of their party, and the system ultimately produces general election choices among equally flawed candidates (see Table 5-3). Additionally, they argue, contemporary nomination procedures maintain an enfeebled two-party system while making it difficult for other parties or independents to organize and field candidates in November.

The 1992 election produced some major changes in the nomination process and threatened even more. The 19 percent national vote secured by Perot in 1992 provided him, or any party he might establish, a regular place on both primary and general election ballots in six states. (After the 1994 elections, the party lost its spot on the ballot in two of these states because it did not field candidates.) This means that a "Perot party" could now participate in a primary or hold caucuses on the designated day, with its candidate automatically qualifying for the general election ballot in November. The candidacy also held the potential to elevate Perot to major party status under the Federal Election Campaign Act, which would have meant primary, convention, and general election funding. Conversely, if Perot had received major party status by receiving 25 percent or more of the November vote, the Democratic or Republican vote might have fallen below 25 percent, which would have relegated them to minor party status.

The 1996 election promises additional change in the rules and procedures of presidential nomination. Further front-loading of delegate selection for the major party conventions has brought the nation to the brink of a national primary. Additional gains by independents or third-party candidates will further open the nomination process to their participation.

But what will ultimately guide this change is voter satisfaction with the choices presented in November. It is inevitable that a significant level of dissatisfaction with the candidates would focus further attention on the nomination system that produced them.

The fact that presidents are not elected by popular votes but by gaining a majority in the electoral college is generally of little consequence, but reform of this dimension of the presidential selection process also receives periodic support. The electoral college usually reaffirms the popular verdict on the candidates. However, when the electoral college has overruled this verdict or narrowly avoided altering it, talk of reform has moved to center stage. Critics have argued that the electoral college is an archaic remnant of past American politics and that popular vote pluralities or majorities should suffice to elect presidents. In fact, in 1979 a majority of the Senate voted for a constitutional amendment abolishing the electoral college and establishing direct popular election of the president. The amendment, however, fell short of the required two-thirds vote.

In 1960, 1968, and 1976 shifts of relatively few popular votes would have left no candidate with an electoral vote majority or would have provided an electoral vote majority to the candidate who had not received the most popular votes (see Table 5-4). With support declining for the two major parties, these possibilities increase greatly, as the 1992 campaign attests. As a result, the electoral college is currently at the center of a brewing crisis.

As with so many other electoral rules and procedures that may need fixing, Congress is either unable to reach consensus on what to do or is increasingly reluctant to impose electoral change upon the states. This essentially means that most recent activity related to the electoral college reform has occurred on the state level. In 1991 Nebraska became the first state in two decades to alter the customary winner-take-all allocation of its electoral votes. Several other states are currently debating a similar move.

A Tricky Business

The laws, customs, and practices of presidential politics are not set in stone. Indeed, most of them have undergone considerable change and continue to be scrutinized with a critical public eye. When some practice becomes intolerable, changes are proposed, debated, and often implemented.

Several dimensions of American electoral change, however, make change an increasingly tricky business. First, the decentralized nature of American politics invites a variety of players to participate in election reform. National parties, state parties, state courts, state legislatures, the Supreme Court, Congress, and the Federal Election Commission, to name but a few, all share responsibility for shaping election laws. As a result, uniform and consistent policy making is rare. Congress, for example, may reject the notion of altering or abolishing the electoral college, but individual states may move to change the allocation schemes of their electoral votes.

Second, all changes have consequences. Many consequences of electoral changes are expected, if not targeted, while others are unforeseen. For example, modifications in the early 1970s in the Democratic rules for selecting delegates to the convention opened the presidential selection process to groups that had been excluded. However, they also drastically reduced representation of elected officials. As a result, the party nominated a presidential candidate without the direct involvement of its congressional delegation—those individuals whom a president would most need to formulate and implement a legislative program. The front-loading of delegate selection for the major party nominating conventions in 1996 could have the positive effect of reducing the disproportionate influence of small groups of voters in states such as Iowa and New Hampshire. On the other hand, by compacting the formal race for the nomination to approximately six weeks in February and March, candidates will have less time to reveal themselves to the American pub lic. As a result, a less complete portrait of a nominee will emerge via the media to the national public.

In this regard, the possibility increases that a party will nominate a candidate who is subsequently revealed to be flawed. The prospect, then, is for a lengthy period of public evaluation and intense media scrutiny from March, when the nomination has been secured, to August, when the candidate will be formally nominated. This also provides a lengthy window of opportunity for potential independent and third-party candidates to test the waters and distribute nomination petitions. In sum, the unforeseen can be as much a problem for election reform as the abuses the reforms seek to eliminate.

Finally, election reform has become increasingly politicized. Although reform of any nature is never devoid of politics, proposed changes in election rules and practices now are an integral part of both presidential campaign strategies and the competition between the two national parties.

Candidates consciously seek to manipulate primary and caucus schedules and the allocation of convention delegates in their favor. Each national party has its own stance on campaign finance that unabashedly serves its own purposes. Most problematic is the increasing production of election rules and practices that serve candidate and partisan ends at the expense of broader principles used to justify these very changes.

Any changes proposed or made in election rules will not be the last. No decade has passed without proposed changes in the presidential selection process being discussed. In some ways, the laws, customs, and practices of this process are a natural focus for the struggle over valued resources in American society because they govern the election of the individual most responsible for the distribution of these resources. In this respect, good citizenship and effective politics share at least one requirement—understanding the rules of the presidential selection process.

Table 5-1   Voting-Age Population Registered and Voting, by State, 1992

State	Voting-age population		State	Voting-age population	
	registered	voted		registered	voted
Alabama	77.5%	55.2%	Massachusetts	72.6%	60.2%
Alaska	79.8	65.4	Michigan	89.0	61.8
Arizona	71.4	54.1	Minnesota	95.8	71.6
Arkansas	74.5	53.8	Mississippi	88.1	52.8
California	66.6	49.1	Missouri	79.3	62.0
Colorado	80.1	62.7	Montana	90.4	70.1
Connecticut	77.1	63.8	Nebraska	81.5	63.4
Delaware	64.8	55.2	Nevada	64.2	50.0
District of Columbia	74.3	49.6	New Hampshire	77.6	63.1
Florida	61.8	50.2	New Jersey	68.3	56.3
Georgia	64.2	46.9	New Mexico	64.1	51.6
Hawaii	52.3	41.9	New York	67.6	50.9
Idaho	82.3	65.2	North Carolina	73.2	50.1
Illinois	77.0	58.9	North Dakota	b	67.3
Indiana	76.2	55.2	Ohio	80.3	60.6
	82.1	65.3	Oklahoma	98.9	59.7
	74.4	63.0	Oregon	79.7	65.7
	74.7	53.7	Pennsylvania	65.6	54.3
	76.5	59.8	Rhode Island	71.4	58.4
	103.2 [a]	72.0	South Carolina	57.3	45.0
	66.2	53.4	South Dakota	89.3	67.0

Table 5-1   *Continued*

State	Voting-age population registered	voted	State	Voting-age population registered	voted
Tennessee	72.1	52.4	Washington	73.7	59.9
Texas	67.3	49.1	West Virginia	70.8	50.7
Utah	84.5	65.2	Wisconsin	c	69.0
Vermont	89.4	67.5	Wyoming	73.0	62.3
Virginia	63.1	52.8			

Source: Committee for the Study of the American Electorate.

[a] Registration figures for Maine reflect more voters than the total state voting-age population.
[b] No registration.
[c] No statewide registration.

Table 5-2   Funding Sources for Major Party Nominees, in millions of dollars

	1988 Bush	Dukakis	1992 Bush	Clinton
Primary elections				
Contributions from individuals				
Less than $500	$ 4.9	$ 7.2	$ 5.3	$14.0
$500–$749	2.7	4.2	2.6	3.8
$750–$1,000	15.0	8.2	19.8	7.6
Contributions from PACs	0.7	—	—	—
Matching funds	8.4	9.0	10.1	12.5
General election				
Grant	46.1	46.1	55.2	55.2
Compliance fund	6.0	3.7	4.3	6.0
Coordinated party expenditures	8.3	8.3	10.2	10.2
Independent expenditures	12.8	0.7	3.4	0.5
Partisan communications	0.1	2.0	—	2.4
Other funding sources				
Leadership PACs	11.2	—	—	—
National party soft money	22.7	25.0	36.2	31.6

Source: Federal Election Commission.

Note: — = not used as precampaign vehicle by candidate that year.

Table 5-3   Turnout in Major Party Primaries, 1972–1992

Year	Democratic primaries	Republican primaries
1972	19.6%	8.1%
1976	17.5	11.1
1980	15.4	11.0
1984	16.4	6.6
1988	15.9	8.6
1992	13.6	8.3

Source: Committee for the Study of the American Electorate.

Note: Turnout is reported only for states that held Democratic or Republican primaries in every presidential election year from 1972 to 1992.

Table 5-4   Close Calls in the Electoral College, 1960, 1968, 1976

Election	Party (result)	Electoral college vote	Change in popular vote that would have caused a deadlock	Deadlocked electoral college vote that would have resulted
1960	Democratic (elected)	303	4,430 in Illinois and 4,992 in Missouri	263
	Republican (defeated)	219		259
	Independent (defeated)	15		15
1968	Republican (elected)	301	30,631 in New Jersey, 10,245 in Missouri, and	268
	Democratic (defeated)	191	12,158 in New Hampshire	224
	American Independent (defeated)	46		46
1976	Democratic (elected)	297	6,383 in Delaware and 5,559 in Ohio	269
	Republican (defeated)	240		269

Source: Presidential Elections, 1789–1992 (Washington, D.C.: Congressional Quarterly, Inc., 1995).

Exercises

1. Review the registration laws and the ʼr turnout in the 1996 presidential election in ʼtate and locality. What impact did these ʼe on voter participation? Should these ʼanged? If so, how?

ʼiew the impact of the National ʼion Act of 1993 ("Motor Voter") locality. Did it make a differ-

3. Using data in Table 5-1, identify two states with disparate registration rates. What might explain these differences?

4. Select any subgroup in the American population (women, African Americans, or Hispanics, for example) and trace changes in registration and suffrage requirements that have had an impact upon their political participation throughout U.S. history.

5. Organize a debate with one side arguing that voting is a right and the other arguing

that voting is a privilege. As part of the debate, identify and support registration procedures that correspond with each side's particular conception of voting.

6. Identify the laws in your state governing access to the November ballot for third-party or independent presidential candidates. Are these laws appropriate or unfair? Explain.

7. Using information contained in Chapters 2 and 5, debate whether the federal campaign finance law, as it applies to presidential campaigns, has worked. How has the law affected the role of money in presidential campaigns? How could the law be improved? Should it be abolished?

8. Conduct a class election in three stages, with one-third of the class voting in fifteen-minute intervals. While the first and second groups vote, reporters from the class should interview those who are voting and, at the conclusion of the round of voting, announce the results to the entire class. After the election is completed, students who voted in the second and third groups should discuss whether the publicized results of the interviews affected their preference or their desire to vote. What does your discussion suggest about the current media practice of declaring a winner of the presidential race before all polls have closed?

9. Identify a critical event which influenced the outcome of either the campaign for nomination or the general election campaign. What was the role of the media in that event? Did the media merely convey information to the public or did they create or fundamentally shape public opinion related to the event?

10. What is the best way to nominate presidential candidates? Why?

11. Several states are currently debating whether they should move from a winner-take-all allocation of electoral votes to a district plan in which candidates receive one electoral vote for each congressional district won and two electoral votes for winning the statewide popular vote. Discuss the merits of this plan and its potential impact on presidential campaigns.

12. Debate the pros and cons of the electoral college.

13. Identify one law, custom, or practice related to the presidential election process and review potential catalysts that might prompt its alteration or abolition. For example, a deadlocked electoral college might prompt a public outcry for change in this institution.

14. Review the impact of the much accelerated (front-loaded) selection of delegates for the 1996 major party conventions. Did this change produce expected or unexpected consequences for the presidential selection process?

Additional Sources
Printed Material and Videos

Rosen, Jay, and Paul Taylor Alexander. *The New News v. The Old News: The Press and Politics in the 1990s*. New York: Twentieth Century Fund, 1992. This book contains two essays that describe the changing nature of the mass media and what possible positive roles it can perform in the context of this rapid and dramatic change.

Sorauf, Frank J. *Inside Campaign Finance*. New Haven, Conn: Yale University Press, 1992. This book reviews the history of campaign finance legislation with an eye to the current dynamics of reform. The last chapter focuses on the 1992 election.

"TV Coverage of Candidates' Personal Lives." A video of prominent journalists discussing the appropriate ethical boundaries of campaign reporting. Available from the Purdue University Public Affairs Video Archives.

On-Line Data

"Charlotte's Web Government Reform Issues." This source offers a wide array of information and documents related to reform of the electoral process. Among the many issues discussed are ballot access for third parties and campaign finance.

Access method: World Wide Web

To access: http://www.emf.net/~cr/govreform.htm1

Choose: Most options relate to election reform "Project Vote Smart." This site is devoted to both voter and reporter education. The latter emphasis includes access to the Reporter's Resource Center of Project Vote Smart, which includes discussions of improving the role of the press in the presidential selection process.

Access method: World Wide Web

To access: http://www.vote-smart.org/

Choose: Search for access to the Reporter's Resource Center under "Project Vote Smart Services"

Candidate Profiles

Profiles of thirty-three candidates who have been mentioned as possible presidential or vice presidential nominees follow. In some cases, exercises in the text require the use of information in these biographies. In others, the biographies merely serve as a useful supplement to other material presented in the chapters. Information for these profiles came from a variety of sources, including the subjects themselves, the *Almanac of American Politics*, *Who's Who in America*, and *Who's Who in American Politics*. Official and unofficial on-line data sources of many declared or undeclared candidates also provided information for the following profiles.

(Andrew) Lamar Alexander, Jr.

Party: Republican.

Summary: Alexander is another in a long line of professional politicians hoping to head the government by promising to dismantle it. A dark horse with political and media savvy, he could capitalize on his reputation for plain talk, an impressive campaign staff, and any faltering by Sen. Bob Dole or Sen. Phil Gramm. Alexander, fifty-five, began his campaign by suggesting that Dole, at seventy-three, would be too old to be president. Alexander's liabilities are those that stick to any candidate who rose to prominence in public service, became a million-aire, then campaigned against the very programs he once supported.

Current Position: Attorney.

Date and Place of Birth: July 3, 1940; Knoxville, Tenn.

Previous Government Positions: Legislative assistant to Sen. Howard Baker, 1967–1968; executive assistant to Bryce Harlow, White House Congressional Liaison Office, 1969–1970; Tennessee governor, 1979–1987; secretary, Department of Education, 1991–1993.

Other Positions: Founder, Corporate Child Care Services; partner, Dearborn and Ewing, 1971–1978; president, University of Tennessee, 1988–1991.

Bill Bradley

Party: Democrat/Independent.

Summary: Bradley's surprise announcement in August 1995 that he would not seek reelection to the Senate added yet another wild card to the presidential election. Although he is not yet an independent, his parting condemnation of both parties as out of touch with the American public suggested a move in that direction. While Bradley clearly lacks charisma and a national network of followers, his candidacy could attract enough disaffected Democratic liberals and moderates to damage the president's reelection bid.

Current Position: U.S. senator, 1979– .
Date and Place of Birth: July 28, 1943; Crystal City, Mo.
Previous Government Positions: None.
Other Positions: Member, U.S. Olympic Team, 1964; member, New York Knickerbockers basketball team, 1967–1977.

Edmund G. (Jerry) Brown, Jr.

Party: Democrat/Independent.
Summary: A botched live television appearance during the 1980 presidential campaign forever marked this former two-term California chief executive as "Governor Moonbeam." Brown's unpopular decisions in his second term, his spartan lifestyle, and his flirtations with Eastern mysticism did nothing to move his eclectic, liberal political persona into the American mainstream. After winning the chairmanship of the California Democratic Party in 1989, he ran again for president in 1992. With Brown, anything is possible, including an independent candidacy.
Current Position: Radio talk show host, "We the People."
Date and Place of Birth: April 7, 1938; San Francisco, Calif.
Previous Government Positions: Member, Los Angeles County Crime Commission, 1969–1970; member, Board of Trustees, Los Angeles Community College, 1969–1970; California secretary of state, 1971–1975; California governor, 1975–1983; chairman, California Democratic Party, 1989–1991.
Other Positions: Law clerk to Justice Matthew Tobriner, California Supreme Court, 1964–1965; attorney, Tuttle and Taylor, l966–1969; chairman, California Democratic Party, 1989–1990; founder, We the People, 1993.

Harry Browne

Party: Libertarian.
Summary: The Libertarian Party is counting on voters' discontent with Democrats and Republicans to propel Browne, its likely nominee, onto the presidential ballot in most states. Browne, a best-selling author of doom-and-gloom investment advice, heads a small but growing movement of disaffected, extreme fiscal conservatives and social liberals. Libertarians believe in minimal national defense, oppose gun control, think drugs should be legalized, oppose prayer in schools, and want welfare and Social Security left to the private sector.
Current Position: Financial writer and investment consultant.
Date and Place of Birth: June 17, 1933; New York, N.Y.
Previous Government Positions: None.

Patrick J. Buchanan

Party: Republican/Independent.
Summary: Buchanan challenged President Bush as insufficiently conservative in 1992 and was doing the same to presumed Republican front-runner Bob Dole in the early going of the 1996 campaign. A leading opponent of the North American Free Trade Agreement and of world trade in general, he has left little doubt that he would lead a third party of social conservatives if the Republicans fail to capture the White House and retain control of Congress. His best hope is as an alternative to Sen. Phil Gramm among the GOP's most conservative wing, which is aiming to have veto power over the party's nominee.
Current Position: Author.
Date and Place of Birth: November 2, 1938; Washington, D.C.
Previous Government Positions: Executive assistant to the president, 1969–1973; director, White House communications, 1985–1987.
Other Positions: Editorial writer, *St. Louis Globe Democrat*, 1962–1964; assistant editorial editor, *St. Louis Globe Democrat*, 1964–1966; syndicated columnist, *New York Times* special features, 1975–1978; commentator, NBC Radio Network,

1978–1982; cohost, "Buchanan-Braden Show," WRC-TV, 1978–1983; syndicated columnist, *Chicago Tribune-New York News* syndicate, 1978–1985; moderator, CNN, "Crossfire," 1982–1985; panelist, "The McLaughlin Group," NBC/PBS, 1982–1985, 1988–1992; moderator, "Capital Gang," CNN, 1988–1992.

Robert P. Casey

Party: Democrat.

Summary: Only four weeks after announcing his exploration of a presidential bid, Casey, sixty-three, withdrew, citing the physical toll a campaign might take. (He had undergone a heart and liver transplant in 1993.) As governor of Pennsylvania, Casey badgered the Clinton administration from the right, strongly opposing abortion, a position that caused fellow Democrats to bar him from speaking at the party's 1992 convention.

Current Position: Attorney.

Date and Place of Birth: January 9, 1932; Jackson Heights, N.Y.

Previous Government Positions: Pennsylvania state senate, 1963–1967; Pennsylvania auditor general, 1969–1977; Pennsylvania governor, 1987–1995.

Other Positions: Practicing attorney, 1957–1969.

Bill Clinton

Party: Democrat.

Summary: Having won the presidency with only 43 percent of the popular vote, Clinton rarely rose above that level in polls during his first term. Devastated by the 1994 Republican sweep of nearly every contested midterm election, Clinton was slow in making his case for a Democratic alternative. When he did, the president pulled the rug out from his remaining allies in Congress by agreeing to a very Republican-sounding, budget-balancing agenda. One of the best underdog campaigners in recent years, Clin-

ton will be fighting a recent trend of one-term presidencies and a wave of new Republican voters. But a thriving economy and a hard-hitting campaign against Republican lawmaking, plus a weak opponent, could give Clinton a second term.

Current Position: U.S. president, 1993– .

Date and Place of Birth: August 19, 1946; Hope, Ark.

Previous Government Positions: Attorney general of Arkansas, 1977–1979; Arkansas governor, 1979–1981, 1983–1992.

Other Positions: Attorney, 1981–1982; faculty, University of Arkansas, 1973–1976.

Bob Dole

Party: Republican.

Summary: Dole began as the Republican front-runner, bedeviled only by the tightrope of running both a national campaign and the U.S. Senate. The right wing of the party has never trusted Dole, and to strengthen his appeal, he began adopting conservative ideology as his own. He put together a seemingly impregnable campaign organization bulwarked by popular Republican elected officials in key states. What distinguishes Dole—his experience—is also the biggest drawback in an electorate seemingly angry at professional politicians. Although his age may be an issue, Dole has been effective in assisting presidents of both parties achieve their congressional goals, and voters are familiar with him because of his thirty-five years on the national stage.

Current Position: U.S. senator, 1969– ; Senate majority leader, 1985–1987, 1995– .

Date and Place of Birth: July 22, 1923; Russell, Kan.

Previous Government Positions: Kansas state representative, 1951–1953; Russell County attorney, 1953–1961; U.S. representative, 1961–1969; chairman, Republican National Committee, 1971–1973; Republican vice presidential nominee, 1976.

Other Positions: Attorney, 1953–1961.

Robert K. Dornan

Party: Republican.

Summary: Dornan announced his candidacy as a way of rescuing America from "cultural meltdown." The originator of the POW-MIA bracelets worn by many Americans in the 1970s, he is a former air force pilot and broadcaster and a bombastic member of the House from southern California whose nasty speeches have even offended the Republican House. Dornan has no role in the outcome of the Republican primaries.

Current Position: U.S. representative, 1977–1983, 1985– .

Date and Place of Birth: April 3, 1933; New York, N.Y.

Previous Government Positions: None.

Other Positions: Broadcast journalist, 1965–1969; talk show host, 1969–1973; host and producer, "Robert K. Dornan Show," 1970–1973.

John M. Engler

Party: Republican.

Summary: Engler is the darling of the new "states' rights" movement that believes any social program is best managed not in Washington but in the states. As governor of a heavily urban state, Engler cut property taxes, revolutionized public school funding, wiped out a $1.8 billion debt, and eliminated welfare for adults without children. He is a possible vice presidential candidate.

Current Position: Michigan governor, 1991– .

Date and Place of Birth: October 12, 1948; Mt. Pleasant, Mich.

Previous Government Positions: Michigan state house of representatives, 1970–1976; Michigan state senate, 1978–1991.

Other Positions: None.

Arthur Fletcher

Party: Republican.

Summary: Fletcher, a black Republican who is on the U.S. Civil Rights Commission, was the Nixon administration official who devised the affirmative action hiring plans now in such disrepute among almost all other GOP candidates. He said in 1995 that running for president may be the only way he can get the party leadership's attention on the value of civil rights and affirmative action. With no base of support, Fletcher's candidacy would serve only to raise an uncomfortable issue within the party.

Current Position: Member, U.S. Commission on Civil Rights, 1990– . (Chairman, 1990–1993.)

Date and Place of Birth: December 22, 1924; Phoenix, Ariz.

Previous Government Positions: Special assistant to Washington governor, 1969; assistant secretary of labor, 1969–1971; alternate delegate to the Twenty-sixth Assembly of the United Nations, 1971; deputy secretary of housing and urban development, 1975–1977.

Other Positions: Executive director, United Negro College Fund, 1971–1973; executive director, National Urban League, 1972–1973; consultant, Arthur A. Fletcher Associates.

Malcolm S. (Steve) Forbes, Jr.

Party: Republican.

Summary: Forbes, son of the late legendary magazine publisher, entered an already crowded race for the Republican nomination in September 1995 at the urging of supply-side tax-cutting conservatives impressed with his international business acumen and his political philosophy. Forbes inherits the mantle of Jack Kemp as spokesman for the pro-business wing of the party and brings to his campaign a sizable personal treasury.

Current Position: President and CEO, Forbes, Inc., 1990– .

Date and Place of Birth: July 18, 1947; Morristown, N.J.

Previous Government Positions: President, Somerset County Park Commission,

1981–1991; chairman, Board for International Broadcasting, 1985–1993.
Other Positions: Editor, *Fact and Comment,* 1974; chairman, Forbes Newspapers, 1989– .

Newt Gingrich

Party: Republican.
Summary: Gingrich was coy about any presidential ambitions after the 1994 electoral revolution swept him into the role of national agenda-setter. The new Speaker of the House is a whirlwind of ideas, a futurist, an obsessive political organizer with a huge coterie of loyalists, and a rhetorical howitzer. While he is young and ambitious enough at fifty-two to bide his time, especially if President Clinton is reelected, the attraction of a Colin Powell candidacy to many GOP stalwarts has placed increased pressure on Gingrich to jump into an already crowded Republican race.
Current Position: U.S. representative, 1979– ; Speaker of the House of Representatives, 1995– .
Date and Place of Birth: June 17, 1943; Harrisburg, Pa.
Previous Government Positions: None.
Other Positions: Faculty, West Georgia College, 1970–1978.

Al Gore

Party: Democrat.
Summary: Gore is more popular than President Clinton within his own party, and possibly among the electorate at large. He accepted the vice presidential nomination in 1992 after declining to run a second time for the top spot himself. His work on "reinventing government" and his prominence as an architect of the information superhighway make his future bright for 1996. He is too loyal and politically astute to become the vehicle for a party coup against Clinton, as much as his many friends in Washington and around the country might like.

Current Position: U.S. vice president, 1993– .
Date and Place of Birth: March 31, 1948; Washington, D.C.
Previous Government Positions: U.S. representative, 1977–1985; U.S. senator, 1985–1993.
Other Positions: Reporter, *Nashville Tennessean*; vice president, Tanglewood Homebuilders Inc., 1971–1976.

Phil Gramm

Party: Republican.
Summary: Gramm played a key role in the defeat of President Clinton's health care reform in 1994 and in forcing withdrawal of Surgeon General nominee Henry Foster a year later; he is the nemesis of Senate Majority Leader Bob Dole, openly disagreeing with him on some issues and trying to thwart him on others. Although he began the campaign as the darling of the Republican right, his reluctance to speak out strongly on behalf of that faction's religious and moral agenda seemed to dampen his prospects by mid-1995. Gramm lent his name to the mandatory budget-cutting legislation of the 1980s. The fiscal results were not as he hoped, but Gramm has been in the front ranks of conservative political and economic warfare since.
Current Position: U.S. senator, 1985– .
Date and Place of Birth: July 8, 1942; Fort Benning, Ga.
Previous Government Positions: U.S. representative, 1979–1985.
Other Positions: Faculty, Texas A&M University, 1967–1978; partner, Gramm & Associates, 1971–1978.

John Hagelin

Party: Natural Law.
Summary: Hagelin is the mostly likely nominee of the recently founded Natural Law Party. Combining the American reform tradition with religious zeal, the new party stresses the use of scientific expertise "to seek out,

verify, and demonstrate cost-effective new solutions to critical social problems." The party qualified in 1992 for primary matching funds and Hagelin, the 1992 nominee, was on the general election ballot in thirty-two states, receiving almost 40,000 votes.

Current Position: Director, Institute of Science, Technology and Public Policy, Maharishi University of Management; spokesperson, Citizens for Conflict-Free Politics.

Date and Place of Birth: June 9, 1954; Pittsburgh, Pa.

Previous Government Positions: None.

Other Positions: Scientific associate, European Laboratory for Particle Physics, 1981–1982; research associate, Stanford University Linear Accelerator, 1982–1983; director, National Demonstration Project to Reduce Violent Crime in Washington, D.C., 1993.

Jesse Jackson

Party: Democrat/Independent.

Summary: Jackson hadn't made much noise by mid-1995, but speeches to supporters left little doubt that he was ready to mount a challenge to President Clinton, most likely as an independent candidate. As is the case with many third-party candidates, his role would be to divert the mainstream farther toward the extreme. Jackson's candidacy could be popular among congressional Democrats because of his ability to mobilize minority voters, but his challenge could drive the president farther to the right, especially on affirmative action, denying him critical moderate votes and thus ensuring a Republican victory.

Current Position: Clergyman; civil rights activist; president, National Rainbow Coalition Inc., 1984– ; "shadow senator," District of Columbia, 1991– .

Date and Place of Birth: October 8, 1941; Greenville, S.C.

Previous Government Positions: None.

Other Positions: Ordained Baptist minister, 1968; executive director, Southern Chris-

tian Leadership's Operation Breadbasket, 1966–1971; national president, Operation PUSH, 1972–1983; host, "Jesse Jackson Show," syndicated by Time-Warner, 1990–1991.

Bob Kerrey

Party: Democrat.

Summary: Kerrey sometimes sounds as if he has forgotten he was beaten by President Clinton in the 1992 primaries, becoming one of the president's most virulent economic critics within the party. When he was named chairman of the Democratic Senatorial Campaign Committee, Kerrey disavowed a challenge to Clinton. His somewhat capricious political manner makes him a threat to Clinton's sense of security, but he will probably wait to run when Clinton is not on the ballot.

Current Position: U.S. senator, 1989– .

Date and Place of Birth: August 27, 1943; Lincoln, Neb.

Previous Government Positions: Nebraska governor, 1983–1987.

Other Positions: Pharmacist, 1965–1966; restaurant, sports/fitness enterprises developer, 1972–1982.

Alan Keyes

Party: Republican.

Summary: Keyes is one of a new breed of African American conservatives who are popular on the stump but voiceless within their own party. In Keyes' case, it is the Republican party, which put him up twice for the U.S. Senate in Maryland only to see him get beaten badly both times. He is considered a fringe candidate, and his unimpressive Senate campaigns make it unlikely he would be considered as a vice presidential candidate.

Current Position: Author, commentator.

Date and Place of Birth: August 7, 1950; New York, N.Y.

Previous Government Positions: Foreign service officer, 1978; consular officer, Bombay, India, 1979–1980; desk officer, Zimbabwe, 1980–1981; policy planning staff, U.S. State Department, 1981–1983; U.S. representative to United Nations Economic and Social Council, 1983–1985; assistant secretary of state, 1985–1988.

Other Positions: President, Citizens against Government Waste, 1989–1991; interim president, Alabama A&M University, 1991; radio host, "The Alan Keyes Show: America's Wake-up Call"; columnist, nationally syndicated column.

Lyndon LaRouche, Jr.

Party: Democrat/Independent.

Summary: LaRouche is a perennial candidate whose ideology has run the gamut from far left to far right. He believes in a Federal Reserve Bank conspiracy aided by the Queen of England and Henry Kissinger, proclaims himself the country's leading economist, and denies the existence of the Holocaust. He has a vast fund-raising operation, which helped land him a five-year prison term for mail fraud. He has in the past and may again qualify for federal campaign matching funds.

Current Position: Writer; economist.

Date and Place of Birth: September 8, 1922; Rochester, N.Y.

Previous Government Positions: None.

Other Positions: Management consultant, L. H. LaRouche Research, 1942–1966; founder and contributing editor, *Executive Intelligence Review*, 1974– ; chairman, advisory committee, National Democratic Policy Committee, 1980–1983.

Richard Lugar

Party: Republican.

Summary: Lugar is his party's chief voice on foreign policy in the U.S. Senate, where he has made his mark as a thoughtful,

respected expert on domestic matters as well. He shattered Midwest political shibboleth by proposing sharp cuts in farm subsidies but also proposed doing away with the income tax and replacing it and other levies with a national sales tax. Lugar may be the most intelligent and experienced of the Republican candidates, but he is dogged by public perception that he can't win. Since 1968 Lugar has always been at the top of his party's vice presidential list.

Current Position: U.S. senator, 1977– .

Date and Place of Birth: April 4, 1932; Indianapolis, Ind.

Previous Government Positions: Indianapolis Board of School Commissioners, 1964–1967; Indianapolis mayor, 1968–1975.

Other Positions: Treasurer, Thomas L. Green & Company, 1960–1967.

Sam Nunn

Party: Democrat.

Summary: As the eighth Senate Democrat to announce retirement plans for 1996, Nunn both dimmed Democratic hopes of recapturing the Senate and substantially stirred the already muddied waters of the presidential and vice presidential races. As the Democratic Party's leading expert on defense matters and one of its more conservative members on economics and social policy, Nunn would be a powerful draw to moderate, white, and southern voters on either a Democratic or independent ticket. Although he is not yet a candidate, his parting statement that it is time for him "to follow a new course" left a world of political options open.

Current Position: U.S. senator, 1973– .

Date and Place of Birth: September 8, 1938; Perry, Ga.

Previous Government Positions: Legal counsel to the House Armed Services Committee, 1963; Georgia state representative, 1968–1972.

Other Positions: Attorney, Nunn, Geiger & Rampey, 1964–1973.

H. Ross Perot

Party: Independence.

Summary: Perot's announcement in September 1995 that he would create a new political party in all fifty states merely reaffirmed his desire to run for president again or, at least, play the role of king maker. While it is yet unclear which option he will pursue, Perot's new Independence Party should not be discounted either as a major factor in the 1996 general election or as a voice for change in contemporary American politics. Any list of possible Independence Party presidential candidates should include Bill Bradley, Sam Nunn, Colin Powell, and Lowell Weicker, as well as Perot himself.

Current Position: President, The Perot Group.

Date and Place of Birth: June 27, 1930; Texarkana, Texas.

Previous Government Positions: None.

Other Positions: Salesman, IBM corporation, 1957–1962; founder, chairman, and CEO, Electronic Data System Corporation, 1962–1984; founder, Perot Systems Corporation, 1988– .

Colin L. Powell, Jr.

Party: Independent/Republican.

Summary: Powell is a glib speaker and the nation's most popular military leader since Eisenhower. As an up-by-the-bootstraps success story from Harlem, Powell was tied in the polls with Clinton and Dole in mid-1995 while publicly and frequently leaving his options open. The Democratic Party is not a real option for him with Clinton in office, and Powell is not likely to want to be vice president to Bob Dole. That leaves a strong possibility that he would run, if at all, as an independent from the large center domain of the American electorate.

Current Position: Author.

Date and Place of Birth: April 5, 1937; New York, N.Y.

Previous Government Positions: Special assistant to the deputy director, Office of the President, 1972; senior military assistant, Office of the Deputy Secretary of Defense, 1977–1979; executive assistant to the secretary of energy, 1979; senior military assistant to the secretary of defense, 1983–1986; deputy assistant to the president for national security affairs, 1987; assistant to the president for national security affairs, 1987–1989; Commander in chief, U.S. forces command, 1989; chairman, joint chiefs of staff, 1989–1993.

Other Positions: None.

Dan Quayle

Party: Republican.

Summary: After Quayle's surgery for a blood clot on the lung and for appendicitis, the 1996 race promised him both more time away from his family and a strong Republican field ahead. In February 1995, the former vice president decided it would be too great a burden to run for the Republican nomination. Quayle, however, reemerged in October 1994 when front-runner Bob Dole tapped him to run his political action committee, Campaign America. With $1.7 million in the bank and strong fund-raising ties to Republican conservatives, Quayle should not be discounted as a possible candidate and the 1996 "comeback kid."

Current Position: Executive, Circle Investors, 1993– .

Date and Place of Birth: February 4, 1947; Indianapolis, Ind.

Previous Government Positions: Chief investigator, Consumer Protection Division, Office of Indiana Attorney General, 1970–1971; administrative assistant, Office of the Governor of Indiana, 1971–1973; director, Indiana Inheritance Tax Division, 1973–1974; U.S. representative, 1977–1981; U.S. senator, 1981–1989; U.S. vice president, 1989–1993.

Other Positions: Attorney, associate publisher, *Huntington Herald-Press,* 1974–1976; chairman, Campaign America, 1995– .

Arlen Specter

Party: Republican.
Summary: Specter is running for president almost as a voice against the Christian Right's domination of the Republican Party. To the left of most of his party on many issues, but suspect among women voters because of his strident defense of Clarence Thomas during his nomination to the Supreme Court, the abrasive Specter has little chance of winning the nomination.
Current Position: U.S. senator, 1981– .
Date and Place of Birth: February 12, 1930; Wichita, Kan.
Previous Government Positions: Assistant counsel, Warren Commission, 1964; Pennsylvania state assistant attorney general, 1964–1965; Philadelphia district attorney, 1966–1974.
Other Positions: Partner, Dechert Price & Rhoads, 1956–1966, 1974–1980.

Morry Taylor

Party: Republican.
Summary: Taylor acts and talks like a junior Ross Perot and has inconspicuously begun to capture some former Perot supporters. His self-financed campaign, based on a reputed $40 million fortune, scored a respectable sixth-place finish in the August 1995 Iowa straw poll. Iowa, however, is Taylor's home turf, and it remains questionable whether he can generate any enthusiasm elsewhere for bringing a "businessman's approach" to government.
Current Position: President and CEO, Titan Wheel International, 1983– .
Date and Place of Birth: August 28, 1945; Detroit, Mich.
Previous Government Positions: None.

Other Positions: Marketing and engineering consultant, General Motors.

Tommy Thompson

Party: Republican.
Summary: Thompson was flirting with a presidential bid in mid-1995, long after the field had taken shape. An innovator on welfare and other social issues that formed the basis of the Republican Contract with America, Thompson has influence among party thinkers but is an unknown nationally. If a Republican nominee needs geographic balance, Thompson might be in the running for the vice presidential slot.
Current Position: Wisconsin governor, 1987– .
Date and Place of Birth: November 19, 1941; Elroy, Wis.
Previous Government Positions: Wisconsin state assembly, 1966–1986.
Other Positions: Attorney, 1966–1987; real estate broker, 1970– .

George Voinovich

Party: Republican.
Summary: Voinovich has been quietly successful, both politically and administratively, as governor of Ohio, a historic swing state in presidential elections. He is not running for president in 1996, but the importance of his state and his moderate stance within the party makes him a potential running mate for a more conservative standard bearer.
Current Position: Ohio governor, 1991– .
Date and Place of Birth: July 15, 1936; Cleveland, Ohio.
Previous Government Positions: Ohio state assistant attorney general, 1963–1964; Ohio house of representatives, 1967–1971; Cuyahoga county auditor, 1971–1976; Cuyahoga county commissioner, 1978–1979; Ohio lieutenant governor, 1979; Cleveland mayor, 1979–1989.
Other Positions: None.

Lowell Weicker

Party: Independent.

Summary: Weicker has blazed a thirty-year career as one of the nation's most prominent mavericks. He opposed the Vietnam war, helped block Reagan social and economic initiatives, and formed a third party that elected him governor of Connecticut. A Weicker presidential campaign would potentially appeal to fiscally conservative but socially liberal voters who, as one columnist put it, would be attracted to a candidate who is "large, voluble, and opinionated."

Current Position: Health services company executive; author.

Date and Place of Birth: May 16, 1931; Paris, France.

Previous Government Positions: Connecticut general assembly, 1962–1968; Town of Greenwich selectman, 1964–1968; U.S. representative, 1969–1971; U.S. senator, 1971–1989; Connecticut governor, 1991–1995.

Other Positions: Attorney, 1958–1968; president, Research! America, 1989–1990.

William Weld

Party: Republican.

Summary: Weld's pro-choice and pro-gay rights stands make him the ideal Republican candidate—for many Democrats. But his aristocratic background and independence—he resigned on principle from a high post in the Reagan administration—make him anathema to the forces dominating the Republican Party. He is a potential surprise vice presidential nominee.

Current Position: Massachusetts governor, 1991– .

Date and Place of Birth: July 31, 1945; Smithtown, N.Y.

Previous Government Positions: Minority counsel, U.S. house of representatives judiciary committee, 1973–1974; U.S. attorney for Massachusetts, 1981–1986; assistant attorney general, Department of Justice, 1986–1988;

Other Positions: Partner, Hill & Barlow, 1971–1981; partner, Hale & Dorr, 1988–1990.

Christine Todd Whitman

Party: Republican.

Summary: Since her election as governor of New Jersey in 1993 and her response to President Clinton's State of the Union address little more than a year later, Whitman has emerged as odds-on-favorite to be someone's vice presidential nominee. A tax cutter from the established moderate faction of the Republican Party, Whitman has proposed welfare reform that would not cut benefits to recipients who have additional children.

Current Position: New Jersey governor, 1994– .

Date and Place of Birth: September 26, 1945; New York, N.Y.

Previous Government Positions: Staff assistant, Republican National Committee, 1969–1971; Somerset County Board of Chosen Freeholders, 1982–1988; New Jersey State Board of Public Utilities, 1988–1990.

Other Positions: Newspaper columnist; radio talk show host; teacher.

Pete Wilson

Party: Republican.

Summary: No California governor can be dismissed in presidential discussion, and Wilson, who came from behind to win a second term in 1994, started the presidential race with money and electoral votes. Considered too moderate by Republican activists, he took strident stands against immigration and affirmative action as he prepared to enter the race. Wilson's campaign, however, was dogged by disorganization, miscalculation, and Wilson's own poor health. Only one month after officially declaring his candidacy in August 1995, the governor called it quits. Despite this dismal record, Wilson may nonetheless reemerge as a vice presidential contender if California's fifty-four electoral votes suddenly loom as the key in a potentially close general election.

Current Position: California governor, 1991– .

Date and Place of Birth: August 23, 1933; Lake Forest, Ill.

Previous Government Positions: California assembly, 1967–1971; San Diego mayor, 1971–1983; U.S. senator, 1983–1991.

Other Positions: Attorney, 1963–1966.

Index